ALSO BY BOBBY FLAY

*Bobby Flay's Grilling for Life: 75 Healthier Ideas for Big Flavor
from the Fire* (with Stephanie Banyas and Sally Jackson)

*Bobby Flay Cooks American: Great Regional Recipes
with Sizzling New Flavors* (with Julia Moskin)

*Bobby Flay's Boy Meets Grill: With More Than
125 Bold New Recipes* (with Joan Schwartz)

Bobby Flay's From My Kitchen to Your Table
(with Joan Schwartz)

Bobby Flay's Bold American Food
(with Joan Schwartz)

BOBBY FLAY'S
BOY GETS GRILL

125 REASONS TO LIGHT YOUR FIRE!

BOBBY FLAY

with Julia Moskin

Color Photographs by Gentl & Hyers

Black-and-White Photographs by John Dolan

Scribner
New York London Toronto Sydney

SCRIBNER
1230 Avenue of the Americas
New York, NY 10020

For information about special discounts for bulk purchases,
please contact Simon & Schuster Special Sales:
1-800-456-6798 or business@simonandschuster.com

DESIGNED BY ERICH HOBBING

Text set in Rockwell

Manufactured in the United States of America

10 9 8 7 6

Library of Congress Cataloging-in-Publication Data

Flay, Bobby.

Bobby Flay's boy gets grill : 125 reasons to light your fire / Bobby Flay, with Julia Moskin ;
color photographs by Gentl & Hyers, black-and-white photographs by John Dolan.
p. cm.
Includes index.
1. Barbecue cookery. I. Title.
TX840.B3F52 2004
641.5'784—dc22
2004045264

ISBN-13: 978-0-7432-5481-6
ISBN-10:   0-7432-5481-3

This book is dedicated to my daughter,

Sophie,

who with every passing day teaches me something

even better than just another good recipe.

Love, Daddy

Acknowledgments

My thanks go to:

- Stephanie Banyas
- Julia Moskin
- Beth Wareham
- Rica Allannic
- John Fulbrook
- Jane Dystel
- Gentl & Hyers
- John Dolan
- Neil Manacle
- Christine Sanchez
- Larry Manheim
- Laurence Kretchmer
- Jerry Kretchmer
- Jeff Bliss
- Tara Taylor Beck
- Sally Jackson
- Stephanie March
- Dorothy Flay
- Bill Flay
- The staffs of Mesa Grill and Bolo

And a special thank-you to the teams at Food Network and CBS's *The Early Show*.

Contents

CONTENTS

X

CONTENTS

xi

BEEF, LAMB, PORK, AND SAUSAGES 197

CONTENTS

XV

Preface

One day I woke up and realized that I had become permanently attached to my grill. How could this be? I am a native New Yorker who still lives in the heart of Manhattan. I didn't grow up with a backyard grill. I have yet to see a grill fired up in the middle of Times Square or in front of the Empire State Building, so I couldn't have just picked up my love for outdoor cooking around town.

Open-flame grilling, as well as propane tanks for gas grills, are pretty much illegal here in Manhattan. But, in fact, there's a lot of grilling that goes on in the city. Manhattanites have been secretly grilling for years. I have been to some fabulous parties on some of New York's most picturesque terraces, where the grill, as always, was the life of the party. But we guerrilla grillers don't talk about it a lot. Until now.

Starting with trips to the Jersey Shore when I was a kid, I've always been attracted to the heat and excitement of the grill. When I was a young chef just starting out, I always wanted to work the grill station. When I got lucky enough to open my own restaurant in 1991, I called it Mesa Grill, and the word "grill" first started to get hooked up with my name. The connection of Flay and fire had begun. And then the Food Network called.

I started with the Food Network back in 1996 on a pretty basic show called *Grillin' & Chillin'.* It was just two guys grilling (me and a friend named Jack McDavid); one city style, the other country style. A few years later, a new show, *Hot off the Grill,* let me cook for my friends (indoors, this time).

And now there's *Boy Meets Grill,* where finally I get to grill in the city (not in Manhattan, but right across the river in Queens). I get to show off my New York and the great ethnic cuisines, ingredients, and markets it has to offer: Chinatown, of course; Astoria, Queens (for Greek food); Arthur Avenue in the Bronx (for old-style Italian); lower Lexington Avenue (better known as Curry Hill, for Indian); the flavors go on and on. From barbecue to pizza, Argentine *asados* to Jamaican jerk, summer vegetables to tandoori to Peking duck, everywhere I go, grilling is there.

Grilling in America used to be about hot dogs, hamburgers, and lighter fluid. But now anything goes on the grill—if you like it, you can grill it. You can scatter a dozen whole clams on the grate of a hot grill to steam in their own briny juices; you can simmer chicken, sausages, and mussels in a big pot; you can grill pizza dough for the crispest, tastiest crust; you can add a little smoke to the sweetness of peaches and nectarines by roasting them on the grill for dessert. The question isn't "Can I grill this?" but "Is there any reason not to grill this?" Usually the answer is: Go ahead and try it! Grilling is the best way I know to keep cooking fun and adventurous.

Of course, *Boy Gets Grill* is the sequel to *Boy Meets Grill,* but it has a direction all its own. The new recipes are even simpler and quicker, to reflect how busy life is now. I still want to cook for my friends and family, and grilling fits into that better and better.

In fact, most of the home cooking I do now starts with turning on the grill. Thanks to my hungry friends and my trusty grill, I've realized that grilling isn't just for weekends and parties anymore.

The recipes in this book are meant to be easy to make and (pleasantly) challenging to your sense of taste. They are full of the flavors, textures, spices, and ideas that have shaped who I am as a person and as a cook. Some recipes are new combinations that (I hope) will become staples in your kitchen. Some are classics that are perfect when adventure seems a little more than you want.

I hope you'll bring out this book whenever you've got your grill cranked up. Don't hesitate to contact me with any grilling question you have at www.bobbyflay.com.

As we all know, New York City has had some difficult days in the last few years, but the spirit of New Yorkers has never paused for a moment. I think the great food we have all over this city is one of the things that brings us together. That was very much in my mind when I was writing this book; I hope you can taste it in the recipes.

Here are at least 125 reasons to light your fire. Most important, have a great time doing it and keep the flame alive.

Bobby Flay
New York City

BOBBY FLAY'S
BOY GETS GRILL

What You Need to Grill (and What You Don't)

The list of things you *don't* need in order to grill great food is a lot longer than the list of what you *do* need. You don't need a grill with a built-in sound system and refrigerator. You don't need lighter fluid. You don't need acres of backyard, a brick oven, or a secret spice rub.

Grilling is the simplest, most basic cooking method there is. All you really need is food and fire. But other things can help: the right ingredients, the right equipment, and the right recipe.

The right ingredients are up to you. Fancy and exotic ingredients don't make great cooks. But no one can make great dishes without great-quality ingredients, so I really encourage you to pay attention to the freshness of every last thing you put in your food, even the basic stuff. This is mostly a matter of shopping carefully and often. The spices in your cabinet lose their flavor after a while. Garlic loses its oomph. "Fresh" fish can be anything but. Make sure that what you use is as good and fresh as it can be, and I swear you will not be sorry that you spent a little extra time at the market.

Here is my list of the right equipment:

* A gas or charcoal grill. I use both, and each one has its advantages. Gas is easy to light, control, and clean. Charcoal is a lot more work, but it gives food a smokiness that gas can never quite imitate. If you use charcoal, you also need a chimney starter (shown on page 2): Don't even talk to me about lighter fluid! And, of course, whatever grill you use, the grate should be reasonably clean, not crusted over.
* A pair of tongs. I find those extra-long grilling tongs hard to use—I feel like the food is too far away from me. So I use regular kitchen tongs for picking up, turning, and moving just about everything. Exceptions are quesadillas and whole fish; for

those, you'll want to have a wide metal spatula, so that you can slide it underneath and carefully turn the whole thing over.

* Brushes. I use good-quality paintbrushes from the hardware store and replace them often, since after a while it's hard to get them clean. Pastry brushes are fine but expensive.

* A workspace. Don't underestimate the importance of having enough room to work. Grilling is much more relaxing when you're not trying to juggle a whole collection of plates and bowls as you do it. If your grill doesn't have enough workspace (and they almost never do), set up a table right next to your grill.

* The right recipes. That's the rest of the book! Don't take them as instruction manuals that need to be followed down to every last detail. Feel free to combine the sauce from one recipe with the fish from another, or change a lemon butter to a garlic butter to fit with the menu you want. Grilling, like eating, is not an exact science: Fires, tastes, and cooks are always different. Trust your own eyes and hands over what's written on the page. Only you can see, feel, taste, and smell what's happening on your grill.

Chimney starter

How Hot Is Hot?

Lighting your fire is a lot easier now than it was just a few years ago. Gas grills are faster and hotter than they used to be. And the chimney starter is the best thing that ever happened to my charcoal grill.

Each recipe in this book tells you exactly how hot a fire you need. Make sure you leave plenty of time to get a good fire going. A gas grill will need about fifteen minutes to preheat. A chimney starter full of charcoal will take about thirty minutes to be ready for cooking. Wait until all the coals are bright orange to dump them into the grill, then give it another five minutes before putting your food on. When the coals are first dumped, they give off a super-hot but uneven heat that isn't what you want for grilling. Let them settle down a little. If you want medium heat, they'll need a little more time to burn down.

Most of the time, I grill over high heat. I like things to move fast, I like the sound and smell of a very hot fire, and I gravitate toward dishes that I can get on and off the grill as quickly as possible. After a while, you'll know without thinking how hot the fire is: high, medium-high, etc. But until then, you can use the time-tested method of holding your hand a few inches—about four—above the grate and seeing how long you can keep it there. I know it sounds a little dangerous, but you'll pull your hand back at just the right moment.

High: 2 counts
Medium-high: 4 counts
Medium: 6 counts
Medium-low: 8 counts
Low: 10 counts

When setting up a charcoal grill for high heat, you often need to keep your options open for grilling at a slightly lower temperature later on. In the recipes you'll often see the direction: Reduce the heat to medium or move to a cooler part of the grill. So you need a fire with a high-heat zone and a medium-heat zone, which is very easy to do. It doesn't matter how you arrange your coals. You can dump them all in the middle and use the center for high heat and the edges for medium heat. Or you can reserve one side of the grill for high and the other for medium, dividing your charcoal and putting fewer coals on one side. Use the hand-test method to check the temperature before putting the food on the grate.

Grilling geeks divide grilling into "direct-heat" and "indirect-heat" categories. The methods I've just described are for direct heat, where all the heat for cooking is coming directly from the coals. But in a couple of cases, such as the whole turkey and the smoked beef brisket, you'll be using indirect heat, where you tinker with the setup of your grill to make it act like an oven, with heat coming from the top, bottom, and sides. Indirect heat is for when you want to cook something slowly on the grill, usually a large piece of meat or a whole bird that would not cook all the way through with direct heat. If you need to use it, the setup will be explained in the recipe.

How Do You Know When It's Done?

The most challenging thing about grilling is knowing when to stop!

I get a lot of questions about doneness, even from experienced grillers. How do I know when chicken is cooked through? What about fish—is it the same? How about lamb—do I need to use a meat thermometer? As with all cooking, it's a matter of taste, experience, and staying cool under pressure.

Anyone who grills needs to master getting the food off the fire when it's cooked just right—not too much, not too little, and allowing for a little more cooking to take place after it's off the heat. I cook most meat to medium-rare, and most fish and chicken a little bit beyond that to "just cooked through."

"Medium-rare" means that the center of the food is barely cooked, but not raw. Medium-rare meat is dark pink, not red and chewy, in the center. Medium-rare fish, such as tuna, is still translucent in the center.

"Just cooked through" means that the center of the food is lightly cooked and still juicy and tender. The flesh you see there should be opaque, not translucent.

Without X-ray vision, how do you know what's going on in the center of the meat? Here are the testing guidelines that I find myself using constantly at the grill:

Rule #1: Don't start testing the food the minute you put it on the heat! This includes picking it up to see if it's done on the bottom, moving it around, and turning it over every ten seconds. Put the food down and give it a chance to cook. This will allow it to sear on the bottom so that it naturally pulls away from the grate and doesn't stick. If you try to move the food before it's seared on the bottom, it will definitely be stuck.

Rule #2: Don't cut into your food to see if it's done. For one thing, it doesn't really work, since you can't get a good look at the inside. For another, it lets the juices come pouring out and the food dries out on the grill. Which leads us to . . .

Rule #3: The best way to test most food is by pressing on it with your finger. If you do this every time you grill, you'll learn quickly how to tell what a perfectly cooked steak or fish fillet feels like. Since you can poke your food as often as you want (unlike sticking a knife into it, which you can only do once), you're much more likely to get the food off the grill at just the right moment.

Rule #4: As meat cooks, it becomes firmer and firmer to the touch. A rare steak feels a little squishy; a medium steak feels springier; a well-done steak feels as taut as a trampoline. The rule of "the longer it cooks, the firmer it gets" also holds true for poultry and fatty fish like tuna and salmon. White fish is a little different, because it firms up quickly, then relaxes and becomes flaky when it's done. As you get more and more experienced, you'll learn exactly what your favorite food should feel like when it's done.

Rule #5: Meat and whole birds should "rest" off the heat for at least a few minutes before you slice or serve them. What does this mean? Put them aside in a warm place, uncovered, and leave them alone. And why are you doing this? Well, without getting too technical about anatomy or chemistry, if you cut into the flesh right as it comes off the heat, the hot juices will run out all over your cutting board. If you wait a few minutes to let them cool just a bit, they'll stay in the meat. You may feel the food is getting cold, but actually it's still cooking. The exceptions are boneless poultry and fish, for they lose heat quickly and should be served immediately.

Rule #6: When in doubt, it's better to undercook than overcook. You can always put food back on the fire if you need to.

Bobby's Guide to Steak

In my twenty years as a chef I've cut, marinated, dry-rubbed, seared, grilled, sliced, and dined on more head of cattle than I like to think about, and steak is still one of my favorite foods. Even with all the fabulous recipes in the world (and in this book!), there are times when you just want to grill a really good steak with some salt and pepper. But how do you get the right cut for the occasion? I know there's a lot of confusion out there about steak cuts, probably because different places and different butchers use different terms for the same cuts of meat. There are hundreds of cuts out there labeled "steak."

Whatever the cut, choosing a great steak is about two things: flavor and texture. A good butcher will be able to give you both in one piece of meat. Whenever possible, I buy from a butcher shop, but meat from a supermarket meat counter can be just as good. The only thing to avoid completely is meat that's prepackaged in plastic trays. The whole point of aging steak is to dry it out, to let the flavors concentrate and improve the texture. Plastic turns the meat wet and swampy.

The best meat is USDA Prime-grade or Certified Black Angus, which is consistently of great quality. But if it's not available or too expensive, Choice meat is fine and sometimes even excellent. Steak fanatics talk a lot about "marbling," the white fat that is distributed through the red muscle, but actually you don't want to see too much of it. Those big streaks of fat won't melt all the way into the steak as it cooks. (Like it or not, that's where most of the flavor comes from.) For maximum juice, you're looking for fine streaks of fat throughout. And a nice thick layer around the outside doesn't hurt either; it keeps the edges from drying out on the fire.

The following cuts are my personal favorites. Any one of them can simply be rubbed with plenty of salt and pepper and grilled over a very hot fire. Thin steaks cook quickly over high heat with a nice crust on the outside and pink meat inside. For thick steaks, you may need to lower the heat after the initial searing so that the inside can cook through without burning the outside. I like to serve steak sliced to show off that brown, beefy crust and the tender, pink meat inside. But always wait five minutes before cutting a hot steak; the juices will stay in the meat instead of running all over your cutting board.

A thick **ribeye** is your perfect summer evening steak, a total crowd-pleaser. It's easy to cook; the fat keeps it nice and juicy and delivers lots of flavor. This is the vehicle for your wildest spice rubs and spiciest barbecue sauces.

The **porterhouse** is the most impressive steak you can serve, period. You get the best of all worlds: flavorful sirloin on one side, butter-soft filet on the other, and a good big bone for the dog. It's the same cut as the **T-bone;** porterhouse just happens to be the part of the cut where the filet is fattest. With a magnificent cut like this, I sometimes hold the spices and just rub a little butter (yes, butter) on the meat, then cook it to medium-rare, no further.

Shell steak and **strip steak** come from the same cut as the porterhouse—the top loin, right in the steer's midsection. They are a little smaller but still juicy, boneless, well marbled, and much less pricey. For steak salads or a casual dinner, they're a great choice.

When it's looks you're after or for an elegant presentation, **filet mignon** is what you want. Filets mignons are just slices of tenderloin. Lots of people like filet mignon because it's small, perfectly shaped, easy to eat, and you can't see any fat on it at all. It has fine texture but not a whole lot of flavor, so I always use an extra-heavy hand with the seasonings.

Flank steak, skirt steak, and **hanger steak** are hits of pure beef flavor. You can do anything to these cuts. I like to marinate them in powerful aromatics like soy, red wine, garlic, ginger, chiles, and they just get better. Cook them to almost medium (rare will be too chewy), then slice them thin, always against the grain, so that the texture of each slice is tender. These are the best for wrapping in tortillas with one of my relishes, and they make great steak salad.

Basic Procedures and Ingredients

ROASTING PEPPERS

Peppers can be roasted on a grill over high heat, turning them over and around until the skin is blackened all over. This gives the best flavor and texture. Or they can be oven-roasted: Preheat the oven to 400 degrees F. Rub the whole peppers with olive oil, place on a baking sheet, and roast, turning once, for about 20 minutes, until softened and blackened.

Transfer the blackened peppers to an airtight container (or use a plastic bag or bowl covered with plastic wrap). Close tightly and set aside for 5 minutes (this helps steam the skins loose). Cut the peppers in half and use your fingers to remove the stems, seeds, and peels. It's a messy job, but don't be tempted to do it under running water—you'll lose all the flavorful oils.

For the best flavor, use the roasted peppers right away, but they can be covered and kept refrigerated for several days.

ROASTING GARLIC

Preheat the oven or toaster oven to 300 degrees F. To roast a whole head of garlic, cut off the top third of the head. For individual garlic cloves, leave whole (do not peel). Rub the garlic with olive oil and wrap tightly in foil. Roast 45 minutes to 1 hour until very soft. Squeeze the pulp from the skins. To squeeze a whole head of garlic, press on the bottom with your thumbs as though you are trying to turn the head inside out; the pulp will slip out of the skins. Pick out any bits of skin and chop or purée in a food processor. Use immediately or cover tightly and refrigerate for several days.

TOASTING SPICES

I toast whole spices, such as cumin and fennel seeds, right before adding them to a dish. Toasting releases the fragrance and cranks up the flavor. Heat a small heavy skillet over medium-low heat, then add the spices. Toss them in the pan until fragrant, 2 to 3 minutes. Watch them carefully, as they can burn suddenly.

TOASTING NUTS AND COCONUT

Just before adding them to a dish, toast nuts to bring their flavor back to life; it works like a charm. Preheat the oven to 350 degrees F and spread the nuts on a sheet pan. Toast 6 to 10 minutes, until fragrant and slightly browned. Check them often, as they can burn quickly. When you just need a small amount, up to ½ cup or so, you can do it in a toaster oven. The method for toasting flaked coconut is the same; shredded coconut should be toasted at 325 degrees F.

CHILES

I enjoy experimenting with different chiles, but if you don't have the kind a recipe calls for, you can always still make the dish. In general, dried chiles can be substituted for each other, and the same goes for fresh. But they all vary hugely in terms of hotness, so when substituting, it's always best to start with a little bit and go from there.

Ancho chiles are dried poblanos (see below), very dark red with a spicy raisin flavor. They are fruity, with moderate heat, and I use them often.

Arbol chiles are dried chiles, small, tapered, and very hot. I use them when I want a pure hit of chile heat.

Cascabel chiles are dried chiles with a great combination of fruity, earthy, and tealike flavors, and medium heat.

Chipotle chiles are smoked jalapeños (see below) with fiery and smoky tastes. They

are available dried or preserved in adobo, a vinegar sauce, and a little goes a long way. For chipotle purée, see below.

Habanero and **Scotch bonnet chiles** are among the hottest of all chiles, but I love their fruitiness. They're both small with a rounded bell shape and range from light green to orange and red, depending on ripeness. If you can't find them, use serranos (see below) in their place.

Jalapeño chiles are about 3 inches long, widely available, and have a pure, fresh, hot flavor. They range from green to red, depending on ripeness. The green ones are hotter.

New Mexico chiles are usually dried. These large chiles have a deep, roasted flavor and moderate heat.

Poblano chiles are usually used fresh. They look like long, flattened, dark green bell peppers. They provide medium heat and lots of fresh pepper flavor.

Serrano chiles are slender, about 2 inches long, and very hot. They can be green or red, depending on ripeness; the green ones are hotter.

CHIPOTLE PURÉE

To make chipotle purée, buy canned chipotles in adobo (see above) and purée the chiles with the sauce in a blender or food processor. Covered and refrigerated, chipotle purée keeps for weeks.

SIMPLE SYRUP

This is very useful to have around, especially in the summer, to sweeten iced tea, lemonade, and cocktails. Make some and you'll never have to watch all the sugar settle to the bottom of your glass again. Combine equal amounts of sugar and water in a saucepan over medium-low heat. Cook gently, swirling the pan occasionally, just until the sugar dissolves and the mixture is clear. Pour into a glass bottle and store in the refrigerator; it will keep nearly indefinitely.

YOGURT

Plain yogurt is great for making creamy dips, lush sauces, and marinades. I use thick yogurt from Greece that's available in ethnic markets and at Trader Joe's. But it's also very easy to strain yogurt for a thicker consistency at home. Start with whole-milk yogurt for the best flavor; fat-free yogurt will not work. Line a strainer with paper towels, set it over a bowl to catch liquid, and pour the yogurt in. Refrigerate for about 4 hours, letting the liquid drain out of the yogurt into the bowl. Discard the liquid. One and one-quarter cups of regular yogurt will yield about 1 cup thick yogurt. Covered and kept refrigerated, it will keep as long as regular yogurt.

OILS

Although you might think that chefs use only the finest extra-virgin olive oil in their kitchens and at the grill, that's not always how it goes. Extra-virgin is perfect for salads or dishes where the oil is one of just a few key ingredients and its flavor is very important. But for most grilling purposes—oiling the top of a quesadilla or the skin of a whole fish—pure olive oil is just fine. Save the good stuff for another time. When I don't want to add the flavor of olive oil to a dish, I use a neutral-tasting vegetable oil, usually canola.

COOL
DRINKS

Extra-Spicy Bloody Marys

We serve hundreds of these every Sunday at Mesa Grill, where brunch might just be my favorite meal of the week—relaxed, happy, and spicy! In fact, I've noticed that people in New York like brunch so much that it's spilling over into Saturday too. Bloody Marys are too good for just one day.

4 cups tomato juice
¾ cup vodka
4 dashes hot sauce
2 dashes Worcestershire sauce
2 pinches of celery salt
Juice of 2 large lemons
¼ teaspoon freshly ground black pepper
Ice
Thin celery ribs, with leaves
1 jalapeño chile, stemmed, seeded,
    and slivered

1. Combine the tomato juice, vodka, hot sauce, Worcestershire sauce, celery salt, lemon juice, and pepper in a pitcher. Refrigerate until ready to serve, up to 4 hours.

2. Pour over ice and garnish each glass with a celery rib and 2 slivers of jalapeño.

Serves 4; can be doubled for 6 to 8

Mango-Mint Iced Tea

This is the kind of cold drink I like to sniff out in New York's ethnic cafés, served in summertime with a great samosa or the perfect spicy empanada. Tamarind, mint, date, and hibiscus are just a few of the exotic, cooling teas you can grab to sip as you walk those torrid sidewalks. Mangoes and mint are perfect with so much of my food, whether the influence is Cuban, Mexican, Southwestern, Asian, or Indian. This iced tea is the real thing—nonalcoholic, delicious, cool, smooth, and festive.

2 quarts cold water
8 high-quality black tea bags
2 cups mango nectar or juice
Sugar
¼ cup fresh mint leaves
Ice
Mango slices or mint sprigs

1. Bring the water to a boil, then pour over the tea bags in a large heatproof pitcher. Steep until the tea is dark, about 5 minutes. Remove the tea bags and add the mango nectar. Add sugar to taste and stir until it is dissolved. Refrigerate until ready to serve, up to 8 hours.

2. Just before serving, stir in the mint leaves. Pour over ice and garnish with a mango slice or mint sprig. Serve immediately.

Serves 4 to 6

White Peach Sangria

Instead of mimosas, serve this golden sangria, with sunny orange, pineapple, and peach flavors, the next time you're cooking brunch for a crowd. You can even make it the night before—it'll only get better.

1 ripe, large white or yellow peach

1 bottle (750 ml) dry white wine,
    preferably a Spanish table wine

1 cup orange juice, preferably fresh

1 cup pineapple juice, preferably fresh

$\frac{1}{3}$ cup brandy

$\frac{1}{4}$ cup triple sec

3 cups sliced peaches, oranges, lemons,
    limes and/or apples

$\frac{1}{4}$ cup simple syrup (optional; page 12)

Ice (optional)

1. Peel the peach and remove the pit. Put the peach in a blender with a few tablespoons of water, just enough to make the mixture blendable, and purée until smooth. Transfer to a pitcher. Add the wine, orange and pineapple juices, brandy, triple sec, and half of the fruit and stir to mix. Taste for sweetness, adding simple syrup if needed. Refrigerate for at least 8 hours and up to 24 hours.

2. When ready to serve, strain out the fruit that's been sitting in the pitcher and discard. Stir in the remaining fruit and serve straight up or over ice.

Serves 4 to 6

Rosé Sangria

I drink lots of chilled, dry rosé in the summer. I find that white wine can't always stand up to the flavors of grilled food, but red is just too heavy on a hot day. Rosé has the perfect balance, and just looking at that pink, frosty wineglass cools me off. When I want something more celebratory than a plain rosé, I make this light sangria. Use a dry rosé, in the French or Spanish style, rather than a sweet white Zinfandel.

1 bottle (750 ml) dry rosé,
preferably Spanish or French
1 cup orange juice, preferably fresh
½ cup brandy
½ cup triple sec
¼ cup simple syrup (page 12), or more to taste
3 cups sliced oranges, lemons, limes, apples,
and blackberries or blueberries
Ice (optional)

1. Combine the wine, orange juice, brandy, triple sec, and simple syrup in a large pitcher. Taste for sweetness, adding more simple syrup if needed. Add half of the fruit and refrigerate for at least 8 hours and up to 24 hours.

2. When ready to serve, strain out the fruit that's been sitting in the pitcher and discard. Stir in the remaining fruit and serve the sangria straight up or over ice.

Serves 4 to 6

Mojitos

New York has some fabulous new bars that take cocktails as seriously as food—with "bar chefs" who use only fresh juices and ingredients to make all their drinks. A few even use fresh-squeezed sugarcane juice, instead of sugar, for sweetening their mojitos; that's how they were originally made in Cuba. But I use plain old superfine sugar (superfine dissolves in cold drinks; granulated doesn't).

**4 teaspoons superfine sugar or simple
    syrup (page 12)**
8 sprigs fresh mint
1 lime, quartered
1 cup light rum
Ice
1 liter club soda

Combine 1 teaspoon sugar and 2 mint sprigs in each of 4 tall (highball) glasses. Using the back of a spoon, mash the mint leaves into the sugar. Squeeze 1 lime quarter into each glass, then pour in ¼ cup rum. Add ice cubes and top off with club soda. Serve immediately.

Serves 4

White Peach Margaritas

I learned to appreciate white peaches in Venice, Italy, mostly by drinking Bellinis at Harry's Bar. (It's a tough job, but someone's got to do the research.)

White peaches have a soft, sweet flavor that's less tart than that of yellow peaches. This margarita is best without salt.

2 ripe large white or yellow peaches
1 cup silver (clear, unaged) tequila
¾ cup peach schnapps
¼ cup fresh lime juice
Ice

1. Peel and pit one of the peaches. Put it in a blender with a few tablespoons of water, just enough to make the mixture blendable, and purée until smooth. Transfer to a pitcher and mix in the tequila, schnapps, and lime juice.

2. Thinly slice the remaining peach. Pour the margarita over ice, garnishing each drink with a slice of peach. Serve immediately.

Serves 4

Pineapple-Mint Tequila Fizz

Fizzy, cold drinks are especially refreshing when you're eating (or making) grilled dishes. The fresh mint and crushed ice remind me of the incredible freshness of the classic mint juleps I drink at the Kentucky Derby, but this is lighter.

1¼ **cups silver (clear, unaged) tequila**
1½ **cups pineapple juice, preferably fresh**
1½ **cups lemon-lime soda**
¼ **cup chopped fresh mint leaves,**
     plus 6 to 8 whole sprigs for garnish
Crushed ice
Fresh pineapple wedges

Combine the tequila, pineapple juice, soda, and chopped mint in a pitcher. Pour into glasses over crushed ice and garnish each drink with a mint sprig and a pineapple wedge stuck over the rim. Serve immediately.

Serves 6 to 8

Fresh Lemonade with Tequila and Mint Sprigs

Lemon, tequila, and mint are just the kind of tart, cool flavors that I crave with grilled food. They blend together happily in a highball glass. Rum can come to the party instead if tequila's flavor doesn't suit your menu.

2 cups fresh lemon juice
1 cup simple syrup (page 12),
    or more to taste
4 cups water
1 cup silver (clear, unaged) tequila
    or light rum
¼ cup fresh mint leaves,
    plus 8 whole sprigs for garnish
Ice

1. Pour the lemon juice into a large pitcher and add the simple syrup and water. Stir and taste for sweetness, adding more simple syrup if needed. Stir in the tequila and mint leaves. Refrigerate for at least 30 minutes before serving.

2. Pour over ice in tall glasses, garnishing each glass with a mint sprig.

Serves 8

DIPS, PIZZA, FLATBREADS, AND QUESADILLAS

Charred Corn Guacamole

What did we do before guacamole came on the scene? People can't seem to get enough of it. When I'm doing a grill party, I sneak kernels of my favorite grilled corn into the classic "guac" recipe. The snap and sweetness of corn is great with silky avocado and crisp red onion. Serve with warm corn tortillas or chips.

4 ears corn, silks removed but husks left on,
    soaked in cold water for at least
    10 minutes
Mild vegetable oil, such as canola
Salt and freshly ground black pepper
4 ripe Hass avocados, halved, pitted,
    peeled, and cut into small dice
½ red onion, finely chopped
1 to 3 serrano chiles (depending on
    how hot you like your guacamole),
    seeded and finely chopped
Juice of 2 limes, or more to taste
2 tablespoons olive oil
¼ cup chopped fresh cilantro leaves

1. Heat your grill to high (page 3).

2. Place the wet corn on the grill, close the grill hood, and cook for 15 to 20 minutes, until steamed through and hot but still crisp (test by carefully piercing with a knife). Remove from the grill and reduce the grill heat to medium (page 3).

3. As soon as the corn is cool enough to handle, remove the husks. Brush the corncobs with vegetable oil, season with salt and pepper, and grill on all sides until the kernels are lightly charred (browned with some black marks but not black all over), about 8 minutes total. Remove from the grill and set aside again until cool enough to handle.

4. To remove the kernels, stand the corn on end in a large bowl and cut downward with a small, sharp knife. Discard the cobs.

5. Mix the remaining ingredients into the corn. Season to taste with salt, pepper, and additional lime juice if needed. *(The guacamole can be made a few hours in advance, covered, and kept refrigerated.)*

Serves 8

Roasted Green Chile–White Bean Dip

When you're grilling for a bunch of people, it's important to have something on hand to serve as soon as they arrive—my friends always seem to be starving. I make savory dips like this one in advance, so that everyone has something to eat while I focus on the grilling. Creamy white beans and fresh-roasted green chiles are great together and make a good change from the usual salsa. Serving good-quality tortilla chips with plenty of corn flavor makes all the difference. Try to find the ones made with natural cornmeal and sea salt.

> **1 pound dried white beans, soaked overnight**
>   **and drained, or 2 (19-ounce) cans white beans,**
>   **rinsed and drained**
> **6 cloves garlic, peeled, or 3 cloves, minced,**
>   **if using canned beans**
> **2 large poblano chiles, roasted, peeled,**
>   **and seeded (page 9)**
> **1 cup olive oil**
> **Salt and freshly ground black pepper**
> **Fresh cilantro leaves**

1. If using dried beans, combine the soaked beans and 6 garlic cloves in a large saucepan and add cold water to cover by 1 inch. (If using canned beans, skip to step 2.) Bring to a boil, reduce the heat, and simmer until soft, 1 to 1½ hours, adding boiling water as needed to keep the beans covered. Drain in a colander.

2. Combine the beans, garlic, and chiles in a food processor and process until coarsely mashed. With the motor running, pour in the olive oil and process until smooth. (If you don't have a food processor, you can use an electric mixer, but the dip will not be as smooth.) Season to taste with salt and pepper and transfer to a medium bowl. *(The dip can be made a day in advance, covered, and kept refrigerated. Bring to room temperature before serving.)* Just before serving, garnish with cilantro leaves.

Serves 8

Sour Cream Salsa

Here are two popular favorites, sour cream–onion dip and salsa, together in one bowl. You'll be surprised how different it tastes—and how fast it disappears! I like this creamy dip best without tomato, but you can add diced plum tomatoes at the last minute if you prefer. And if you like things spicy, add a few dashes of your favorite hot sauce. Serve with good-quality tortilla chips (page 28).

2 cups sour cream
1 small red onion, finely chopped
2 jalapeño chiles, finely chopped
2 tablespoons fresh lime juice
¼ cup finely chopped fresh cilantro leaves
Salt and freshly ground black pepper

Combine the ingredients in a medium bowl and season to taste with salt and pepper. *(The dip can be made a few hours in advance, covered, and kept refrigerated.)* Serve cold.

Serves 4 to 6

Feta and Scallion Dip
with Olive Oil and Lemon

Feta is salty, tangy, and creamy—three of my favorite flavors. There are lots of different kinds; at my supermarket, I can buy French, Bulgarian, Greek, and Danish fetas! Here's how to decide: The closer you get to Greece, the stronger the cheese. Some of them are pretty powerful. Any feta is good in this chunky dip; the scallions add fresh green flavor and a nice color.

Pocketless pita breads are moist and chewy, so they grill up really nicely. You can also use the flatbread recipe on page 38 or grill regular pita breads.

**12 scallions, dark green and pale green
parts only, chopped, plus 1 scallion,
thinly sliced, for garnish**
**¼ cup extra-virgin olive oil, plus extra
for brushing the pitas**
2 teaspoons grated lemon zest
2 tablespoons fresh lemon juice
1 pound feta (see headnote), crumbled
Salt and freshly ground black pepper
6 pocketless pita breads

1. Combine the chopped scallions, oil, lemon zest, and lemon juice in a food processor and process until smooth. (If you don't have a food processor, you can use an electric mixer or a wooden spoon instead, but the dip will not be as smooth.) Add the feta and process until smooth. Scrape the mixture into a serving bowl. *(The dip can be made up to this point a few hours in advance, covered, and kept refrigerated. Bring to cool room temperature before serving.)* When ready to serve, season to taste with salt and pepper and garnish with the sliced scallion.

2. Heat your grill to high (page 3).

3. Brush the pitas with a little oil and sprinkle with salt and pepper. Grill the pitas for 1 minute on each side, until lightly browned. Remove from the grill and cut each pita into 8 wedges for serving. Serve warm with the dip.

Serves 8

Thick Yogurt with Lemon-Basil Pesto and Grilled Bread

I discovered thick, creamy yogurt from the Mediterranean at the wonderful food stores on Atlantic Avenue in Brooklyn, a neighborhood that used to be a magnet for immigrants from the Middle East. Rich and substantial enough to be a dip, it's a world away from the thin, watery yogurt we're used to getting; the texture is closer to sour cream. If you can't buy this incredible stuff where you live (it's often labeled "Greek style" or "Mediterranean style"), you can easily duplicate the texture by draining regular whole-milk yogurt in a strainer; see page 12 for the procedure.

In this recipe, when you swirl the intense green pesto through the white yogurt, it creates a cool-looking marbled effect that also tastes amazing.

2 cups packed fresh basil leaves

2 tablespoons pine nuts

3 cloves garlic, chopped

1 teaspoon grated lemon zest

½ cup extra-virgin olive oil,
plus extra for brushing and serving

Salt and freshly ground black pepper

2 cups thick yogurt (page 12)

1 baguette or "peasant"-style loaf,
cut into ½-inch-thick slices

1. Combine the basil, pine nuts, garlic, and zest in a food processor or blender and process for 30 seconds. With the motor running, slowly add the oil and process until smooth. Season to taste with salt and pepper. *(The pesto can be made a day in advance, covered, and kept refrigerated.)*

2. Place the yogurt in a serving bowl and swirl about ½ cup of the pesto into the yogurt, making a marbled effect with a thin rubber spatula or a fork; do not mix. Just before serving, drizzle the dip with a few tablespoons olive oil.

3. Heat your grill to high (page 3).

4. Brush the bread slices on both sides with olive oil and sprinkle with salt and pepper. Grill the bread for 1 minute on each side, until lightly charred. Serve warm with the dip.

Serves 6 to 8

Smoky Red Pepper and White Bean Dip

This classic from Mesa Grill, my restaurant in Manhattan, is pale red and smoky sweet, with a lush creamy texture. Puréed beans are so silky smooth that I actually forget I'm eating something healthy.

Use canned beans to make this recipe super easy. Here's a little secret: Canned beans often have a better texture than home-cooked ones. Canned beans are pressure-cooked right in the cans, and that makes them creamier than simmered ones. Or if you have a pressure cooker, use that to cook dried beans. Serve with high-quality tortilla chips (page 28).

> 1 pound dried white beans, soaked overnight
>   and drained, or 2 (19-ounce) cans white beans,
>   rinsed and drained
> 4 cloves garlic, peeled, or 2 cloves, minced,
>   if using canned beans
> 2 large red bell peppers, roasted, peeled,
>   seeded, and diced (page 9)
> 3 tablespoons red wine vinegar
> 1 tablespoon chipotle purée (page 12)
> 1 tablespoon honey
> Salt and freshly ground black pepper
> ¼ cup chopped fresh cilantro leaves

1. Combine the soaked beans and garlic in a large saucepan and add cold water to cover by 1 inch. (If using canned beans, skip to step 2.) Bring to a boil, reduce the heat, and simmer until soft, approximately 1 to 1½ hours, adding boiling water as needed to keep the beans covered. Drain in a colander; do not discard the garlic.

2. Combine the roasted peppers, vinegar, and chipotle purée in a food processor and process until smooth. (If you don't have a food processor, you can use an electric mixer instead, but the dip will not be as smooth.) Add the beans and garlic to the mixture and process until smooth. Add the honey and season to taste with salt and pepper.

3. Transfer to a bowl and garnish with chopped cilantro. *(The dip can be made a few hours in advance, covered, and kept refrigerated. Bring to room temperature before serving.)* Serve with tortilla chips.

Serves 6 to 8

Tomato Bread with Prosciutto

When you have good bread and ripe tomatoes at hand, make this simple, authentic Spanish snack for your guests as they arrive. You can even use good-quality canned tomatoes if your locally grown ones aren't ready yet. Any cured meat or even salami is tasty as long as it's sliced paper thin. In fact, the tomato bread is really good all by itself.

6 very ripe plum tomatoes
    or 3 beefsteak tomatoes, seeded
    and chopped
4 cloves garlic, finely chopped
¼ cup olive oil, plus extra for brushing
Salt and freshly ground black pepper
1 tablespoon fresh thyme leaves, finely chopped
8 slices ciabatta or other crusty,
    country-style bread, about ½ inch thick
8 thin slices prosciutto, serrano,
    or Smithfield ham

1. Combine the tomatoes, garlic, olive oil, and salt and pepper to taste in a food processor or blender. Purée until smooth, transfer to a bowl, and stir in the thyme. Let sit at room temperature for at least 30 minutes. *(The purée can be made up to a day in advance, covered, and kept refrigerated. Bring to room temperature before serving.)*

2. Heat your grill to high (page 3).

3. Brush the bread slices on both sides with olive oil and sprinkle with salt and pepper. Grill the bread for 1 minute on each side, until lightly charred. Remove the bread from the grill and generously brush each slice on one side with the tomato purée. Top each one with a slice of prosciutto and serve.

Serves 4; can be doubled for 6 to 8

Grilled Flatbread
with Cucumber-Yogurt Salad
and Toasted Walnuts

In the summer, I can't get enough of the clean, bold flavors of Greek food. It's probably because the whole cuisine evolved around grilling! The classic Greek cucumber salad, tzatziki, is cool but not mild—it always has a good bite of garlic to it. The flavor is fantastic with the smokiness of grilled lamb, fish, or even plain grilled bread.

You can serve grilled pita bread instead (page 30), but making flatbread on the grill is easy. It does take a while, but most of the time you are just leaving the dough alone to rise. And the fresh, yeasty flavor is so satisfying! The repeated risings make the breads light and crackly.

FOR THE FLATBREAD:
$1\frac{1}{2}$ **cups warm water**
$\frac{1}{2}$ **teaspoon dry yeast**
4 cups all-purpose flour
$\frac{1}{2}$ **teaspoon salt, plus extra for sprinkling**
2 tablespoons olive oil, plus extra
      for brushing
Freshly ground pepper

1. Mix the water and yeast in the bowl of a mixer fitted with a dough hook and let stand for 15 minutes.

2. Start the mixer at medium-low speed and slowly add 2 cups of the flour. When this flour is lightly mixed in, mix for about 1 minute more. Let rise, covered with a kitchen towel, until doubled in size, 1 to 2 hours.

3. Start the mixer again at medium-low speed and mix in the salt and oil. Add the remaining flour $\frac{1}{2}$ cup at a time, mixing after each addition just until the flour is incorporated. Remove the dough from the bowl and knead for a few minutes until the dough is smooth. Place in an oiled bowl, cover with a kitchen towel, and let rise in a warm place until puffed, about $2\frac{1}{2}$ hours.

4. Divide the dough into quarters and roll into balls with your hands. Cover with a kitchen towel and let rise in a warm place for another 30 minutes.

5. Heat your grill to high (page 3).

6. On a lightly floured surface, roll each ball into a 6-inch round. Brush the rounds with olive oil and season with salt and pepper.

7. Grill the breads for 2 to 3 minutes, turn them over, and grill for another 1 to 2 minutes, until lightly charred, firm, and crisp. Remove from the grill and brush with more olive oil. Cut into wedges for serving.

FOR THE SALAD:

1 large cucumber, peeled, seeded, and finely grated

2 cups thick yogurt (page 12)

4 cloves garlic, finely chopped

Juice of 1 lemon

3 tablespoons finely chopped fresh mint leaves

¼ cup finely chopped fresh dill leaves, plus extra for garnish

Salt and freshly ground black pepper

½ cup toasted walnuts (page 10), finely chopped

Combine the cucumber, yogurt, garlic, lemon juice, mint, and dill in a medium bowl and season to taste with salt and pepper. *(The cucumber salad can be made a few hours in advance, covered, and kept refrigerated.)* Just before serving, garnish with dill and chopped walnuts. Serve with the warm flatbread.

Serves 6 to 8

Grilled Pizza with Grilled Sausage, Peppers, Onions, and Oregano Ricotta

Rolling out pizza dough is one of the first cooking skills I learned, thanks to my after-school job at Mimi's Pizza on Lexington Avenue. Sausage and peppers was always my favorite combination. People are sometimes intimidated by the idea of grilling pizza, but it's actually very easy—a lot easier than grilling chicken in fact! Precooking the crusts on the grill is the key. If you don't want to make your own pizza dough, you can often buy it fresh from a local pizzeria or refrigerated at the supermarket.

This tomato-less pizza can make a whole meal, packed with Italian flavor, alongside my favorite tomato-mozzarella salad (page 58) and a platter of lemony grilled octopus (page 132).

**1 recipe flatbread dough (page 38)
or 16 to 20 ounces fresh or refrigerated
pizza dough (see headnote)**

Olive oil

Salt and pepper

**10 ounces Italian sausages, hot, sweet,
or a combination of the two**

**1 large red onion, sliced
into ¼-inch-thick rounds**

**2 large yellow bell peppers, stemmed,
seeded, and quartered lengthwise**

**2 large red bell peppers, stemmed, seeded,
and quartered lengthwise**

**8 ounces (1 cup) whole-milk ricotta,
preferably sheep's milk**

1 tablespoon chopped fresh oregano leaves

8 ounces fontina cheese, coarsely grated

Fresh basil and/or flat-leaf parsley leaves

1. Heat your grill to medium-high (page 3).

2. Divide the dough into quarters and roll out on a lightly floured surface until thin but still stretchy (you don't want it so thin that it will easily tear). The pizzas can be approximately 6-inch rounds, squares, or whatever shape you prefer.

3. Brush the crusts with olive oil, season with salt and pepper, and grill for 2 to 3 minutes, until golden brown on the bottom. Turn them over and grill until crisp, 1 to 2 minutes more. Remove from the grill and set aside on a large cookie sheet (or two if needed), or sheet of foil that will fit on your grill. Leave the grill on.

4. Grill the sausages on both sides until golden brown and cooked through, about 10 minutes on each side. Brush the onion and peppers with oil and season with salt and pepper. Grill the onion and peppers until soft and browned, 3 to 4 minutes on each side.

5. Remove the sausages from the grill (leave the grill on), let rest for 5 minutes, then slice ¼ inch thick. Remove the onion and separate into rings. Remove the peppers and slice each quarter lengthwise in half.

6. Mix the ricotta and oregano in a small bowl and season to taste with salt and pepper.

7. To assemble the pizzas, divide the fontina cheese among the crusts (leave the crusts on the cookie sheet or foil). Divide the sausages, onion, and peppers over the cheese. Transfer the cookie sheet to the grill, close the cover, and grill until the cheese has melted, 2 to 3 minutes. When the pizzas are almost done, raise the lid and put a few dollops of the ricotta mixture on each one. If using two cookie sheets, do this step in two batches.

8. Remove from the grill and sprinkle with the basil. Let rest for 3 minutes before serving, then serve the pizzas whole or in slices.

Serves 4 as an entrée; 6 to 8 as an appetizer

Crispy Bacon and Corn Quesadillas with Avocado–Cherry Tomato Relish

Quesadillas are one of my favorite things to grill for a bunch of people. You can get all the ingredients together in advance, then just stack them up and stick them on the grill when you're ready to serve. They're great as lunch, brunch, or a substantial appetizer before a grilled dinner. This quesadilla has all the flavors of summer—tomato, corn, onion, avocado—but it's the bits of smoky bacon, lightly charred on the grill, that make this quesadilla irresistible.

The strong, sweet flavor of miniature tomatoes stands up really well to grilled food. Grape tomatoes have a more oval shape than round cherry tomatoes, and pear tomatoes are shaped like little teardrops. Sweet 100 tomatoes are my favorites, but you can use any kind in this recipe.

FOR THE RELISH:

2 ripe Hass avocados, halved, pitted, peeled, and diced

4 ounces tiny cherry or grape tomatoes (see headnote), halved

½ red onion, thinly sliced

2 jalapeño chiles, seeded and minced

Juice of 1 lime

3 tablespoons mild vegetable oil, such as canola

¼ cup chopped fresh cilantro leaves

Salt and freshly ground black pepper

Combine all the ingredients in a bowl and season with salt and pepper to taste. *(The relish can be made a few hours in advance, covered, and kept refrigerated. Bring to cool room temperature before serving.)*

FOR THE QUESADILLAS:

16 thick slices bacon

3 ears corn, husked

Mild vegetable oil, such as canola

Salt and freshly ground black pepper

12 (6-inch) flour tortillas

2 cups grated Monterey Jack cheese

1 cup grated white Cheddar cheese

2 scallions, thinly sliced

2 teaspoons ancho chile powder

Cilantro leaves

1. Heat your grill to medium (page 3).

2. Grill the bacon, laying it across the grate of the grill, for 4 to 5 minutes on each side, until golden brown and crispy but not blackened. Remove the bacon to a plate lined with paper towels (leave the grill on), let cool slightly, and crumble or coarsely chop.

3. Brush the corn all over with oil and season with salt and pepper. Grill the corn on all sides until lightly charred (browned with some black marks, but not black all over), about 8 minutes total. Remove from the grill and set aside (leave the grill on). To remove the kernels, stand the corn on end in a large bowl and cut downward with a small, sharp knife. Discard the cobs.

4. Place 8 of the tortillas on a flat work surface. Divide the cheeses, scallions, crumbled bacon, and charred corn among the tortillas and season with salt and pepper.

5. Make 4 quesadillas by stacking the filled tortillas by twos, then placing one of the remaining plain tortillas on top. Press lightly to help the quesadilla hold together. Brush the tops of the quesadillas with oil and sprinkle with the ancho powder. Carefully place them oiled side down on the grill and cook until golden brown on the bottom, about 2 minutes. Carefully turn the quesadillas over with a large metal spatula, close the grill hood, and continue cooking for 1 to 2 minutes, until the cheese has melted and the tortillas are crisp.

6. Remove the quesadillas from the grill, cut into quarters, and top each quarter with a dollop of the avocado relish. Garnish with cilantro leaves. Serve immediately.

Serves 4

Grilled Quesadillas with Sweet Corn, Grilled Shrimp, and Jalapeño Pesto

I've found myself putting corn and shrimp in the same dish at Mesa Grill more times than I can count. Somehow these two sweet, tender ingredients go together really well, especially with the freshness of jalapeños. (I always love to feel that chile zap! It wakes your whole mouth up.) This super-popular quesadilla has been part of the menu at Mesa ever since we opened in 1991.

The traditional cheese for quesadillas in Mexico is *queso chihuahua,* a mild, smooth cheese that's perfect for melting. Our Monterey Jack, combined with a bit of Cheddar for tanginess, is the perfect substitute.

FOR THE PESTO:

8 jalapeño chiles, roasted, peeled, seeded, and chopped (page 9)

2 cups fresh cilantro leaves

2 cloves garlic, chopped

2 tablespoons pine nuts

½ cup olive oil

Salt and freshly ground black pepper

Combine the jalapeños, cilantro, garlic, and pine nuts in a food processor or blender and process until smooth. With the motor running, slowly pour in the oil and blend until emulsified. Season to taste with salt and pepper. Scrape the mixture into a bowl and set aside. *(The pesto can be made up to a day in advance, covered, and kept refrigerated. Bring to room temperature before serving.)*

FOR THE QUESADILLAS:

3 ears corn, husked

12 (6-inch) flour tortillas

2 cups grated Monterey Jack cheese

1 cup grated white Cheddar cheese

1 sweet onion, such as Vidalia or Walla Walla,
    thinly sliced into rounds
2 tablespoons finely chopped fresh thyme leaves, plus extra for garnish
Salt and freshly ground black pepper
Olive oil
16 large shrimp, shelled and deveined

1. Heat your grill to medium (page 3).

2. To remove the kernels from the corncobs, stand the corn on end in a large bowl and cut downward with a small, sharp knife. Discard the cobs.

3. Place 8 of the tortillas on a flat work surface. Divide the cheeses, corn, onion, and thyme among the tortillas and season with salt and pepper.

4. Make 4 quesadillas by stacking the filled tortillas by twos, then placing one of the remaining plain tortillas on top. Brush the tops of the quesadillas with olive oil.

5. Brush the shrimp with olive oil and season with salt and pepper. Place on the grill and grill just until pink and lightly charred, about 2 minutes on each side. Remove and set aside. Leave the grill on.

6. Carefully place the quesadillas oiled side down on the grill and cook until golden brown on the bottom, about 2 minutes. Carefully turn the quesadillas over with a large metal spatula, close the grill cover, and continue cooking for 2 minutes more, until the cheese has melted and the tortillas are crisp.

7. Remove the quesadillas from the grill and cut into quarters for serving. Top each quarter with a tablespoon of pesto and a grilled shrimp. Garnish with thyme leaves and serve immediately.

Serves 4

Grilled Quesadillas with Sliced Steak, Blue Cheese, and Watercress

This quesadilla takes me right back to my favorite New York steakhouse, Peter Luger in Brooklyn, where the martinis are perfectly dry and the steaks are perfectly aged. I always like to have a salad with blue cheese when I eat a good steak. This quesadilla—spiked with peppery watercress and sweet onion—makes a simple summer dinner when you serve it with a platter of ripe tomato slices.

1 (12-ounce) strip steak (page 8)
Salt and freshly ground black pepper
12 (6-inch) flour tortillas
2 cups grated Monterey Jack cheese
1 cup crumbled blue cheese
½ sweet onion, such as Vidalia or Walla Walla,
    thinly sliced
Mild vegetable oil, such as canola
6 ounces watercress, chopped

1. Heat your grill to high (page 3).

2. Season the steak with plenty of salt and pepper. Grill until browned and crusty on the bottom, about 4 minutes. Turn the steak over and continue cooking until medium-rare (page 5), 3 to 4 minutes more. Remove from the grill, let rest for 5 minutes, and thinly slice.

3. Reduce the grill heat to medium (page 3).

4. Place 8 of the tortillas on a flat work surface. Divide the cheeses and onion among the tortillas and sprinkle with salt and pepper.

5. Make 4 quesadillas by stacking the filled tortillas by twos, then placing one of the remaining plain tortillas on top. Brush the tops of the quesadillas with oil. Carefully place them oiled side down on the grill and cook until golden brown on the bottom, about 2 minutes. Carefully turn the quesadillas over with a large metal spatula, close the grill

cover, and continue cooking for 1 to 2 minutes, until the cheese has melted and the tortillas are crisp.

6. Remove the quesadillas from the grill and cut into quarters for serving. Top each quarter with a couple of slices of steak and a generous pinch of watercress. Serve immediately.

Serves 4

Grilled Quesadillas with Feta, Spinach, and Olive-Lemon Relish

I love quesadillas so much that I'm always experimenting with new cheeses to stuff into them. The idea for a feta quesadilla led me to other Greek staples, like spinach and black olives. Together they make a surprisingly authentic-tasting Mediterranean appetizer. Don't forget the ouzo.

I like to buy my feta right out of the tubs at the great cheese shops on Manhattan's Ninth Avenue, many of which are owned by Greeks—they get the best feta. Feta should not be tightly wrapped in plastic; if you buy it that way, unwrap it when you get home and store it in a bowl with some salt water and a little milk.

FOR THE RELISH:

½ **red onion, thinly sliced**
¾ **cup chopped oil-cured black olives**
2 tablespoons grated lemon zest
2 tablespoons red wine vinegar
¼ **cup extra-virgin olive oil**
Salt and freshly ground black pepper

Mix the onion, olives, zest, vinegar, and oil together. Season to taste with salt and pepper. *(The relish can be made a few hours in advance, covered, and kept refrigerated. Bring to room temperature before serving.)*

FOR THE QUESADILLAS:

12 (6-inch) flour tortillas
2 cups grated white Cheddar cheese
1 cup crumbled feta
6 ounces baby spinach
Salt and freshly ground black pepper
Olive oil

1. Heat your grill to medium (page 3).

2. Place 8 of the tortillas on a flat work surface. Divide the cheeses and spinach among the tortillas and sprinkle with salt and pepper.

3. Make 4 quesadillas by stacking the filled tortillas by twos, then placing one of the remaining plain tortillas on top. Brush the tops of the quesadillas with olive oil. Carefully place them oiled side down on the grill and cook until golden brown on the bottom, about 2 minutes. Carefully turn the quesadillas over with a large metal spatula, close the grill cover, and continue cooking for 1 to 2 minutes, until the cheese has melted and the tortillas are crisp.

4. Remove the quesadillas from the grill and cut into quarters for serving. Top each quarter with a spoonful of relish. Serve immediately.

Serves 4

Grilled Quesadillas
with Black Olive Tapenade, Goat Cheese,
and Tomato-Basil Relish

I got addicted to tapenade—a pungent blend of olives, anchovies, capers, and garlic from Provence—when I was invited to cook at the Cannes film festival. On the plane back, I was eating it straight out of the jar! Now, instead of putting out bowls of olives before a grilled dinner, I make this savory quesadilla.

Although you can buy tapenade here in the States, it is incredibly easy to make yourself, and the taste is so much fresher. Tapenade is not quite the same as Italian black olive paste, so don't use that as a substitute—it's too strong.

FOR THE TAPENADE:

1½ cups Kalamata, Niçoise,
or other brined black olives, pitted
2 cloves garlic, chopped
1 tablespoon pine nuts
1 tablespoon anchovy paste
¾ cup olive oil
Salt and freshly ground black pepper

Combine the olives, garlic, pine nuts, and anchovy paste in a food processor or blender and process until coarsely chopped. With the motor running, slowly pour in the oil and process until smooth and emulsified. Transfer to a bowl and season to taste with salt and pepper. *(The tapenade can be made up to a day in advance, covered, and kept refrigerated. Bring to room temperature before serving.)*

FOR THE RELISH:

3 ripe beefsteak tomatoes, cored, seeded,
and diced
½ red onion, thinly sliced
2 cloves garlic, finely chopped

2 tablespoons red wine vinegar

¼ cup extra-virgin olive oil

2 tablespoons finely shredded
  fresh basil leaves

Salt and freshly ground black pepper

Combine all the ingredients in a bowl and season to taste with salt and plenty of pepper. Set aside. *(The relish can be made a few hours in advance, covered, and kept refrigerated. Bring to room temperature before serving.)*

FOR THE QUESADILLAS:

12 (6-inch) flour tortillas

8 ounces fontina cheese, coarsely grated

1 cup crumbled fresh goat cheese

12 fresh basil leaves, finely shredded,
  plus extra whole leaves for garnish

Olive oil

---

1. Heat your grill to medium (page 3).

2. Place 8 of the tortillas on a flat work surface. Spread each of the tortillas with a few tablespoons of tapenade. Divide the cheeses on top of the tapenade and sprinkle with the shredded basil.

3. Make 4 quesadillas by stacking the filled tortillas by twos, then placing one of the remaining plain tortillas on top. Brush the tops of the quesadillas with olive oil. Carefully place them oiled side down on the grill and cook until golden brown on the bottom, about 2 minutes. Carefully turn the quesadillas over with a large metal spatula, close the grill cover, and continue cooking for 1 to 2 minutes, or until the cheese has melted and the tortillas are crisp.

4. Remove the quesadillas from the grill, cut into quarters, and top each quarter with a dollop of the tomato relish. Garnish with basil leaves. Serve immediately.

Serves 4

Grilled Four-Cheese Quesadillas with Roasted Red Peppers and Yellow Tomato-Thyme Salsa

Creamy ricotta cheese and sweet roasted peppers are one of those made-in-heaven pairings. When I was growing up, I was really envious of some kids I knew whose mother was a fantastic Italian cook. She always had a big bowl of fresh ricotta on the table at dinnertime, to eat on bread, to top a tomato salad, or to stir into pasta to make it rich. That's where my love for ricotta cheese began.

The yellow tomatoes I use in the salsa are a little sweeter than red ones, which makes them a good match for the other ingredients.

FOR THE SALSA:

3 ripe yellow tomatoes, seeded and diced

½ red onion, thinly sliced

2 cloves garlic, finely chopped

3 tablespoons white wine vinegar

3 tablespoons extra-virgin olive oil

2 teaspoons finely chopped fresh thyme leaves

2 tablespoons chopped fresh flat-leaf
    parsley leaves

Salt and freshly ground black pepper

Combine all the ingredients in a bowl and season to taste with salt and pepper. *(The salsa can be made a few hours in advance, covered, and kept refrigerated. Bring to room temperature before serving.)*

FOR THE QUESADILLAS:

2 large red bell peppers, stemmed, seeded,
    and quartered

Olive oil

12 (6-inch) flour tortillas

1¼ cups grated Monterey Jack cheese

8 ounces mozzarella cheese, thinly sliced

½ cup freshly grated Parmesan cheese

Salt and freshly ground black pepper

8 ounces whole-milk ricotta cheese

---

1. Heat your grill to high (page 3).

2. Brush the peppers with oil. Grill the peppers until soft and browned, 3 to 4 minutes on each side. Remove from the grill and, when the peppers are cool enough to handle, coarsely chop.

3. Reduce the grill heat to medium (page 3).

4. Place 8 of the tortillas on a flat work surface. Top each tortilla with a few tablespoons Jack cheese, a couple slices mozzarella, and a tablespoon Parmesan. Scatter the red peppers on top and season with salt and pepper.

5. Make 4 quesadillas by stacking the filled tortillas by twos, then placing one of the remaining plain tortillas on top. Brush the tops of the quesadillas with olive oil. Carefully place them oiled side down on the grill and cook until golden brown on the bottom, about 2 minutes. Carefully turn the quesadillas over with a large metal spatula, close the grill cover, and continue cooking for 1 to 2 minutes, or until the cheese has melted and the tortillas are crisp.

6. Remove the quesadillas from the grill, cut into quarters, and top each quarter with a dollop of tomato salsa and a dollop of ricotta cheese. Serve immediately.

Serves 4

VEGETABLE APPETIZERS, SALADS, AND SIDES

Avocado Salad with Tomatoes, Lime, and Toasted Cumin Vinaigrette

This creamy, chunky salad, with huge flavors of tomato, avocado, arugula, cumin, and cilantro, seems to go with almost everything I grill. It's great with all kinds of Latin and Caribbean dishes, and especially with the Cuban-inspired grilled pork tenderloin on page 230.

Make sure to use ripe Hass avocados, which have the best flavor.

FOR THE VINAIGRETTE:

¼ **cup fresh lime juice**

2 **tablespoons rice vinegar**

1 **tablespoon honey**

1 **tablespoon cumin seeds, lightly toasted**
   (page 10)

¼ **cup chopped fresh cilantro leaves**

Salt and freshly ground black pepper

¼ **cup olive oil**

¼ **cup mild vegetable oil, such as canola**

Whisk together the lime juice, vinegar, honey, cumin, cilantro, and salt and pepper to taste in a bowl. Gradually whisk in the oils until emulsified. (Or combine all the ingredients in a jar with a tight-fitting lid and shake very well.) Taste for salt and pepper, adding more if needed. *(The vinaigrette can be made a few hours in advance, covered, and kept refrigerated. Whisk or shake well before serving.)*

FOR THE SALAD:

4 **ripe large tomatoes, cut into large chunks,**
   or 20 cherry tomatoes, halved

2 **ripe large Hass avocados, halved, pitted,**
   peeled, and cut into large chunks

1 **large red onion, thinly sliced**

2 **cups arugula leaves**

1 teaspoon ground cumin

¼ cup fresh cilantro leaves

Gently mix the tomatoes, avocados, onions, arugula, and half the vinaigrette in a large bowl. Taste for vinaigrette, salt, and pepper, adding more if needed. Sprinkle the cumin and cilantro over the top and serve immediately.

Serves 4; can be doubled for 6 to 8 (no need to double the dressing)

Fresh Buffalo Mozzarella with Red and Yellow Tomatoes and Basil Vinaigrette

You haven't really lived until you've tasted totally fresh mozzarella, and you don't have to go to Italy to do it. In New York there are still a few places, like Joe's Dairy and DiPalo's, that make mozzarella every morning. Whenever I go, it's like a little miracle. The difference is unbelievable.

In Italy this salad is often made with water-buffalo milk mozzarella, and I once visited a Vermont cheese maker who raises the animals for this purpose. You can buy fresh, imported *mozzarella di bufala* at many cheese stores, or you can order it online from *www.dairysection.com*. The main thing is, buy the freshest mozzarella you can get your hands on. If you only have access to those shrink-wrapped, salty rubber blocks at the supermarket, use goat cheese instead or leave it out!

FOR THE VINAIGRETTE:

½ **cup fresh basil leaves**
¼ **cup white wine vinegar**
Salt and freshly ground black pepper
¾ **cup olive oil**

Combine the basil and vinegar in a blender, add salt and pepper to taste, and blend until smooth. With the motor running, slowly pour in the oil. Taste for salt and pepper, adding more if needed. *(The vinaigrette can be made a few hours in advance, covered, and kept refrigerated. Whisk or shake well before serving.)*

FOR THE SALAD:

1 pound fresh buffalo or cow's milk mozzarella
    (see headnote), cut into ¼-inch-thick slices
2 ripe large red tomatoes, cut into ¼-inch-thick slices
2 ripe large yellow tomatoes, cut into ¼-inch-thick slices
Fresh basil leaves, thinly sliced
Salt and coarsely ground black pepper

Arrange the cheese and tomatoes in overlapping slices (alternate the colors with a slice of cheese, then a slice of red tomato, and then a slice of yellow tomato) on a platter. Drizzle with the vinaigrette (you may not use all of it) and garnish with basil. Sprinkle with salt and pepper and serve immediately.

Serves 4; can be doubled for 6 to 8 (no need to double the dressing)

Stacked Tomato Salad with Goat Cheese and Tapenade

In the Hamptons where I live in the summer, August is the time for local tomatoes. These days they're likely to be green, purple, striped, and yellow as well as red. (Heirloom tomatoes are fun to play with but not always worth the premium price. In my opinion nothing beats a really perfect ripe beefsteak.)

To keep things interesting, I'm always coming up with different spins on the tomato-mozzarella-basil combination that everyone loves. This one is spiked with a little surprise—a swipe of intense black olive spread. You can use any ripe tomatoes for this recipe; buy *garrotxa* (pronounced gar-O-cha), a creamy, slightly aged Spanish goat cheese that I serve at Bolo, at *www.dairysection.com*.

FOR THE DRESSING:
¼ **cup white wine vinegar**
1 tablespoon Dijon mustard
2 tablespoons honey
¾ **cup olive oil**
Salt and freshly ground pepper
12 basil leaves, thinly sliced

Whisk together the vinegar, mustard, and honey in a medium bowl. Gradually whisk in the olive oil until the mixture is emulsified. Season to taste with salt and pepper and stir in the basil. *(The dressing can be made a few hours in advance, covered, and kept refrigerated. Bring to room temperature before serving.)*

FOR THE SALAD:
4 pounds ripe tomatoes, such as beefsteak
    or heirloom varieties, cut into
    ½**-inch-thick slices**
Tapenade (page 50)

1 pound *garrotxa* **or other creamy, mild,**
    aged goat cheese, thinly sliced
Basil sprigs

Place a tomato slice on a serving plate and spread with a little tapenade. Place a slice of cheese on top and finish with another tomato slice. Repeat, making three tomato stacks on each plate. Drizzle the vinaigrette over the tomato stacks and around the plate. Garnish with basil sprigs and serve immediately.

Serves 6 to 8

Grilled Bread Panzanella

In addition to being addictively delicious, this Tuscan salad could not be easier—or more useful. How often does a fabulous dish also help you use up stale bread? Panzanella is a great starter for a grilled meal but also works well as a side dish: It's starch and vegetable in one. Try this with Butterflied Chicken with Rosemary-Lemon-Garlic Oil, Parmesan, and Black Pepper (page 178).

Because it's slightly dry, the bread absorbs the tangy dressing and the juices from the ripe tomatoes. Grilling the bread first—my addition to the classic recipe—makes it deliciously chewy and smoky.

8 ripe large beefsteak tomatoes, diced

1 small red onion, halved and thinly sliced

2 cloves garlic, finely chopped

¾ cup extra-virgin olive oil, plus extra
   for brushing

¼ cup red wine vinegar

¼ cup chopped fresh basil leaves,
   plus whole sprigs for garnish

Salt and freshly ground black pepper

1 loaf day-old crusty bread, such as ciabatta
   or "peasant" bread, cut into ¾-inch-thick slices

1. Heat your grill to high (page 3).

2. Mix the tomatoes, onion, garlic, oil, vinegar, and chopped basil in a large bowl. Season to taste with salt and pepper and set aside at room temperature for 30 minutes.

3. Brush the bread lightly with olive oil and grill until golden brown and lightly charred, 1 to 2 minutes on each side. Remove from the grill and cut into 1-inch cubes.

4. Mix the bread into the tomato mixture, making sure the bread is well coated with the juices, and transfer the salad to a serving platter. Garnish with fresh basil sprigs and serve immediately.

Serves 8

Fava Bean
and Manchego Cheese Salad

This is Spain in a bowl. A substantial side dish, with fresh beans, sharp cheese, and sweet peppers, it goes well with almost anything that's Mediterranean and grilled. Fresh fava beans are one of the signs of spring in Italy and Spain, but if you can't get them, fresh American lima beans and broad beans work well too. You can even use shucked Japanese *edamame,* fresh soybeans; those have become the easiest ones to find in my neighborhood!

Piquillo peppers are a Spanish specialty, small, dark red, and delicious; you can order them, roasted and packed in oil, from *www.tienda.com.*

1½ **pounds fava beans, shucked,**
   about 2 cups (see headnote)
¼ **cup aged sherry vinegar**
1 **tablespoon Dijon mustard**
½ **cup olive oil**
Salt and freshly ground black pepper
8 **piquillo peppers, drained and finely diced,**
   or 2 red bell peppers, roasted, peeled,
   seeded, and finely diced (page 9)
4 **ounces Manchego cheese, thinly sliced**
   and broken into shards
1 **cup baby salad greens or mesclun**
¼ **cup grated cheese, such as Pecorino Romano,**
   grana Padano, or Parmesan
Chopped fresh flat-leaf parsley leaves

---

1. Bring a large pot of salted water to a boil. Have ready a medium bowl filled halfway with ice water. Add the fava beans to the pot and cook until tender, 2 to 5 minutes. Drain the beans and plunge them into the ice bath, then drain again when cool. Carefully remove the skins and place the beans in a bowl. *(The beans can be prepared a few hours in advance, covered, and kept refrigerated.)*

2. Whisk together the vinegar and mustard in a medium bowl. Gradually whisk in the oil until emulsified and season to taste with salt and pepper. *(The vinaigrette can be made a few hours in advance, covered, and kept refrigerated. Whisk or shake well before serving.)*

3. When ready to serve, add the peppers and Manchego cheese to the fava beans and toss with some of the vinaigrette. Place the greens in another bowl and toss with some of the vinaigrette. Divide the fava bean mixture on serving plates, top with the greens, and sprinkle with grated cheese. Drizzle with a little bit more vinaigrette and garnish with chopped parsley. Serve immediately.

Serves 4; can be doubled for 6 to 8 (no need to double the dressing)

Crunchy Vegetable Slaw with Peanut Sauce and Crispy Noodles

My friend (and once my sous-chef) Patricia Yeo taught me how to make tangy-crisp vegetables in the Asian style—which is somewhere between a salad and a pickle. The key is rice vinegar. Slightly sweet, mild, and delicious, it doesn't make your eyes tear up or your mouth pucker, and now I use it in lots of my vinaigrettes. This easy dressing, full of rich peanut and sesame flavor, is great with crunchy mouthfuls of cabbage, romaine, carrots, fried noodles, and scallion.

I love this with the soy-ginger chicken on page 170, but leave out the peanut butter (that dish is served with a peanut dipping sauce). Add ¼ cup canola oil to the dressing instead.

FOR THE DRESSING:

½ **cup smooth, all-natural peanut butter**

¼ **cup rice vinegar**

2 to 3 tablespoons water

2 teaspoons toasted sesame oil

2 teaspoons soy sauce

Pinch of hot red pepper flakes

1 teaspoon sugar

Whisk together the peanut butter, vinegar, water, sesame oil, soy sauce, pepper flakes, and sugar in a bowl. Taste and adjust the seasonings until you have a good balance of sweet, salt, vinegar, and sesame flavors. *(The dressing can be made a day in advance, covered, and kept refrigerated.)*

FOR THE SLAW:

1 head romaine lettuce, thinly shredded
    crosswise

1 head pale green cabbage, cored
    and thinly shredded

2 carrots, coarsely grated

2 scallions, thinly sliced

1 cup crunchy (fried) chow mein noodles

¼ cup fresh cilantro leaves

Toss the lettuce, cabbage, carrots, and scallions with the dressing and transfer to a large platter for serving. Top with the crunchy noodles and cilantro leaves. Serve immediately.

Serves 8

Jicama Slaw with Lime-Ancho Dressing

I'm always on the lookout for food that can satisfy my need for CRUNCH! Jicama (pronounced HEE-kah-mah), a root vegetable, was one of my favorite discoveries on my first trip to the American Southwest; it arrived there via Mexico. Now you can buy it in many supermarkets across the country; a jicama is about the size of a grapefruit and has a thin brown skin. Crisp as a Granny Smith apple, freshly cut jicama makes perfect slaw.

FOR THE DRESSING:

½ **cup fresh lime juice**

2 tablespoons rice vinegar

2 tablespoons ancho chile powder

2 tablespoons honey

½ **cup mild vegetable oil, such as canola**

Salt and freshly ground pepper

Whisk together the lime juice, vinegar, ancho powder, and honey in a bowl. Whisk in the oil and season to taste with salt and pepper. *(The dressing can be made a day in advance, covered, and kept refrigerated. Bring to room temperature before using.)*

FOR THE SLAW:

1 **(2-pound) jicama, peeled**
  and cut into matchsticks

½ **head napa cabbage, cored and shredded**

2 carrots, coarsely grated

¼ **cup finely chopped fresh cilantro leaves**

Combine the jicama, cabbage, and carrots in a large bowl. Pour the dressing over the jicama mixture and toss to coat well. Mix in the cilantro. Let sit at room temperature for 15 minutes before serving.

Serves 8

Parmesan-Crusted Portobello Mushroom Caps

The meaty tops of portobello mushrooms are the closest thing to steak in the vegetable kingdom, and I love to grill them just like a steak. You can serve this as an entrée to vegetarians or as a great side dish for a crusty ribeye.

White truffle oil can be bought in tiny bottles at most gourmet stores, but it isn't essential to the dish. The truffle oil should have an unbelievably fresh and concentrated perfume of mushrooms; if yours doesn't seem all that fragrant or if it smells at all stale, use good-quality extra-virgin olive oil instead. I'd rather use a great simple ingredient than a mediocre fancy one any day!

⅓ **cup freshly grated Parmesan cheese**
2 tablespoons chopped fresh thyme leaves
Salt and coarsely ground black pepper
4 portobello mushrooms, cleaned and stems removed
Olive oil
4 teaspoons white truffle oil or extra-virgin olive oil

1. Heat your grill to medium-high (page 3).

2. Combine the Parmesan and thyme in a small bowl and season to taste with salt and pepper. Brush the mushrooms on both sides with oil and season with salt and pepper to taste.

3. Place the mushrooms upside down on the grill and cook until golden, 5 to 6 minutes. Turn the mushrooms over and continue grilling until cooked through, 4 to 5 minutes more.

4. When the mushrooms are cooked through, without removing them from the grill, carefully divide the cheese mixture among the mushrooms. Close the cover of the grill and cook just until the cheese has melted, about 30 seconds. Remove to a platter and drizzle 1 teaspoon truffle oil over each mushroom. Serve immediately.

Serves 4; can be doubled for 6 to 8

Grilled Corn on the Cob
with Garlic Butter, Fresh Lime,
and Queso Fresco

Corn is the perfect vegetable for grilling because it comes with a built-in protective wrapper—the cornhusk. The natural moisture in the green husks helps steam and smoke the corn until it's sweet, tender, and full of flavor. In Latin cooking, corn is often sprinkled with lime juice and fresh cheese—queso fresco—for contrast. I've combined that with the American love for butter, butter, and more butter on corn on the cob.

FOR THE GARLIC BUTTER:

12 tablespoons (1½ sticks) unsalted butter, slightly softened

4 cloves garlic, coarsely chopped

Salt and freshly ground black pepper

Combine the butter and garlic in a food processor or with a mixer until smooth. (To mix by hand, let the butter get very soft, then beat in the garlic, finely minced, with a large wooden spoon.) Season to taste with salt and pepper. *(The garlic butter can be made in advance, covered, and kept refrigerated up to 2 days, or frozen for a week. Bring to cool room temperature before serving.)*

FOR THE CORN:

8 ears corn, silks removed but husks left on, soaked in cold water for at least 10 minutes

2 fresh limes, quartered

½ cup crumbled queso fresco or mild feta

1. Heat your grill to high (page 3).

2. Place the corn on the grill, close the grill hood, and cook for 15 to 20 minutes, turning occasionally, until steamed through and hot but still crisp (test by carefully piercing with

a knife). Unwrap the husks from the corn and immediately spread or brush with garlic butter.

3. Squeeze the limes on top and and sprinkle with cheese. Serve immediately.

Serves 4 to 6

Grilled Artichokes
with Smoky Tomato Vinaigrette

I love to indulge in artichokes every spring when they are large, fresh, and plentiful—and when I'm just getting into the grilling groove after the winter. Like corn, artichokes are great with nothing more than melted butter, but sometimes it's fun to mix things up a little. This smoky, tomato-red vinaigrette brings out the earthy flavor of the artichoke, and the colors are great.

FOR THE VINAIGRETTE:

6 plum tomatoes, chopped
¼ cup red wine vinegar
2 teaspoons chipotle purée (page 12)
1 clove garlic, chopped
2 tablespoons chopped fresh basil leaves
½ cup mild vegetable oil, such as canola
Salt and freshly ground black pepper

Combine the tomatoes, vinegar, chipotle, garlic, and basil in a blender and blend until smooth. With the motor running, slowly pour in the oil until emulsified. Season to taste with salt and pepper. *(The vinaigrette can be made a few hours in advance, covered, and kept refrigerated. Whisk or shake well before serving.)*

FOR THE ARTICHOKES:

4 large artichokes
1 lemon, halved
2 tablespoons olive oil, plus extra for brushing
2 tablespoons salt, plus extra to taste
Freshly ground black pepper

1. Trim off the sharp points on each artichoke with scissors and place the artichokes in a large pot. Squeeze in the juice of the lemon and add the olive oil and salt. Fill the pot with enough cold water to cover the artichokes and place a heatproof plate on top of the

artichokes to hold them under the water. Bring to a boil over high heat and boil for 20 to 25 minutes, until tender (test by pulling off a leaf near the base—it should come off easily but with a little resistance). Remove the artichokes from the pot and let cool. *(The artichokes can be cooked a few hours in advance and set aside.)*

2. Heat your grill to medium (page 3).

3. Divide the vinaigrette among 4 small bowls or ramekins. Cut the artichokes lengthwise in half and scrape out the chokes with the tip of a teaspoon. Brush the artichoke halves with olive oil and season with salt and pepper.

4. Grill the artichokes cut side down for 2 minutes, until lightly browned. Turn them over and grill 1 minute more. Remove to serving plates and serve immediately with the vinaigrette.

Serves 4; can be doubled for 6 to 8 (no need to double the dressing)

Grilled Zucchini with Romesco Sauce and Hazelnuts

This is the perfect summer side dish, especially when you have more zucchini than you know what to do with. Romesco sauce, a Spanish classic that I love, is rich with hazelnuts, sweet with red peppers, garlicky, spicy, and smoothed with a binding of bread crumbs and olive oil. And it's easy to make.

FOR THE ROMESCO SAUCE:

4 tablespoons olive oil

1 thick slice white bread, crust removed, cut into small cubes

6 cloves garlic, peeled and left whole

2 red bell peppers, roasted, peeled, seeded, and coarsely chopped (page 9)

2 ancho chiles, soaked in boiling water until soft, seeded, and chopped

2 plum tomatoes, seeded and chopped

¼ cup hazelnuts, lightly toasted (page 10) and chopped

1 tablespoon honey

½ cup red wine vinegar

Salt and freshly ground black pepper

1. Heat 2 tablespoons of the oil in a large skillet over medium-high heat. Add the bread and cook, stirring, until golden brown on all sides, about 5 minutes. Using a slotted spoon, remove the bread to a plate. Add another tablespoon oil to the pan, add the garlic, and cook, stirring, until golden, about 3 minutes. Using a slotted spoon, remove the garlic and place on the plate with the bread.

2. Add the remaining tablespoon oil to the pan; add the peppers, chiles, and tomatoes and cook, stirring, until the tomatoes are just soft, about 10 minutes. Using a slotted spoon, transfer the mixture to a food processor or blender and add the garlic, bread, hazelnuts, and honey. Pour the vinegar into the pan and scrape up any brown bits with a

wooden spoon. Pour the contents of the pan into the food processor and purée until smooth. Season to taste with salt and pepper. *(The sauce can be made a few hours in advance and set aside. Do not refrigerate.)*

FOR THE ZUCCHINI:

3 medium zucchini, cut on the diagonal
into ½-inch-thick slices
¼ cup hazelnuts, lightly toasted
(page 10) and chopped
¼ cup finely chopped fresh chives

---

1. Heat your grill to medium (page 3).

2. Place the zucchini slices in a baking dish, add ½ cup of the romesco sauce, and turn to coat each slice. Grill the zucchini for 3 to 4 minutes on each side, until just cooked through and golden brown. Transfer the zucchini to a platter and top with the remaining romesco. Sprinkle with chopped hazelnuts and chives. Serve immediately.

Serves 4; can be doubled for 6 to 8 (no need to double the sauce)

Coconut-Cashew Basmati Rice Salad

Cooking rice in coconut milk makes it so rich and delicious that it seems almost decadent. I add crunchy cashews, fresh scallions, and chewy coconut to cut through the creaminess. If you happen to see whole coconuts at the store, it's fun to serve this dish inside coconut halves for a party. I'm lucky, for within a few blocks of my house I can buy fresh coconuts at an Indian market, a Latino bodega, or a West Indian grocery store! I love New York.

**4 tablespoons mild vegetable oil,
    such as canola**
1 medium onion, halved and thinly sliced
1 clove garlic, chopped
1 tablespoon grated fresh ginger
Salt
**2 cups basmati rice, rinsed several times
    with cold water and drained well**
1 (14-ounce) can unsweetened coconut milk
2¼ cups water
Freshly ground black pepper
½ cup raw cashews, halved
8 to 12 scallions, thinly sliced (1 cup)
**½ cup grated fresh or shredded unsweetened
    dried coconut**

1. Heat 3 tablespoons of the oil in a medium, heavy saucepan with a tight-fitting lid over medium-high heat. Add the onion, garlic, and ginger, sprinkle with salt, and cook, stirring, until soft, 4 to 5 minutes; do not brown. Add the rice and cook, stirring, for 2 to 3 minutes.

2. Meanwhile combine the coconut milk and water in a medium saucepan and bring to a simmer. Add the hot liquid to the rice, season with salt and pepper, and bring to a boil. Reduce the heat to very low, cover tightly, and let cook undisturbed for about 20 minutes, until the rice is soft and has absorbed all of the liquid.

3. While the rice is cooking, heat the remaining tablespoon oil in a small pan over medium heat. Add the cashews and cook, stirring, until light golden brown. Drain on paper towels and season with salt.

4. When the rice is cooked, transfer it to a large serving bowl and fold in the scallions and coconut, fluffing the rice and breaking up any clumps. Season to taste with salt and pepper. Garnish with the cashews and serve hot or at room temperature. *(The salad can be made a few hours in advance, covered, and set aside at room temperature.)*

Serves 6 to 8

Grilled Vegetable–Saffron Rice Salad

In New York even the smallest souvlaki joints and kebab carts always serve really great rice pilafs with their food. Whether it's simply well-seasoned rice or a jumble of vegetables, nuts, and aromatics, pilaf is a classic side dish for grilled food from Morocco to Spain to Greece. This hearty one, with zucchini, peppers, and asparagus, is my favorite—and it's so rich in flavors and textures that you can eat any leftovers for lunch the next day! Feel free to play around and use different vegetables in season.

FOR THE RICE:

3 tablespoons olive oil

1 Spanish onion, finely chopped

2 cloves garlic, finely chopped

Salt

2 cups long-grain white rice

4 cups water

1 large pinch saffron threads

Freshly ground black pepper

1. Heat the oil in a medium, heavy pot with a tight-fitting lid over medium heat. Add the onion and garlic, sprinkle with salt, and cook, stirring, until soft, 4 to 5 minutes; do not brown. Add the rice and stir to coat the grains of rice with the oil.

2. Meanwhile place the water in a small pot and bring to a boil. Add the saffron and let boil for 1 minute. Stir the saffron water into the rice, season with salt and pepper, and bring to a boil. Reduce the heat to low, cover the pot, and cook undisturbed for 18 to 20 minutes, until the rice is soft and has absorbed all the liquid. Let the rice sit covered for 5 minutes, then fluff with a fork.

FOR THE VEGETABLES:

2 red bell peppers

2 yellow bell peppers

12 spears asparagus, trimmed

1 large zucchini, halved lengthwise
Olive oil
Salt

1. Heat your grill to high (page 3).

2. Brush the vegetables with oil and sprinkle with salt. Grill the peppers until blackened on all sides, then transfer to a bowl and cover with plastic wrap. Let sit for 20 minutes to steam the skins loose and cook the flesh. Peel with your hands (do not do this under running water, or you'll lose the flavorful oils), core, seed, and cut into bite-size pieces.

3. Lay the asparagus crosswise on the grate and grill, turning, until charred and just cooked through, 3 to 5 minutes on each side. Let cool and cut into 1½-inch lengths.

4. Grill the zucchini cut side down until golden brown, 4 to 5 minutes. Turn it over and grill 4 to 5 minutes more, until just cooked through. Cut into bite-size pieces.

TO SERVE:
¾ cup oil-cured black olives, pitted
    and chopped
Extra-virgin olive oil
Aged sherry vinegar
¼ cup chopped fresh flat-leaf parsley leaves
Salt and freshly ground black pepper

Transfer the rice to a large serving bowl and stir in the grilled vegetables and olives. Drizzle with a little olive oil and sherry vinegar, stir, and taste, adding more if needed. Stir in the parsley and season to taste with salt and pepper. Let sit at room temperature for at least 30 minutes before serving if possible. Taste for oil, vinegar, salt, and pepper, adding more if needed, and serve warm or at room temperature. *(The salad can be made a few hours in advance, covered, and set aside at room temperature.)*

Serves 6 to 8

Texmati Rice Salad with Black-Eyed Peas and Roasted Red Peppers

My first job in a restaurant was at Joe Allen's, a classic joint in Manhattan's theater district that was (and is) always packed. It was the early '80s, Cajun and Southern food was suddenly trendy, and I made mountains of hoppin' John, a mix of black-eyed peas and rice, every day. It's a down-home dish, but those fashionable New Yorkers ate it up, with blackened this and barbecued that. It's still a great side for food that's spicy, grilled, or both.

I rediscovered the dish later in Texas, made with Texmati rice, a cross of Indian basmati and Carolina long-grain. Texmati has a nutty taste and cooks up very fluffy and dry.

1½ cups dried black-eyed peas, washed
    and picked over
3 thyme sprigs
6 tablespoons mild vegetable oil,
    such as canola
1 large onion, finely chopped
1½ cups long-grain white rice,
    preferably Texmati
3 cups water
2 red bell peppers, roasted, peeled,
    seeded, and diced (page 9)
8 scallions, thinly sliced
1 tablespoon finely chopped
    fresh thyme leaves
¼ cup finely chopped fresh
    flat-leaf parsley leaves
¼ cup red wine vinegar
3 to 5 dashes hot sauce
Salt and freshly ground black pepper

1. Combine the peas and thyme sprigs in a large pot with enough water to cover by 2 inches. Bring to a boil over high heat, skimming the foam that rises to the top. Cook for 1 to 1½ hours, until the peas are tender, adding more boiling water as needed to keep the peas covered. Drain the peas and keep warm. Discard the thyme.

2. After the peas have been cooking for 1 hour, heat 3 tablespoons of the oil in a medium saucepan with a tight-fitting lid over medium-high heat. Add the onion and cook, stirring, until soft, about 5 minutes; do not brown. Add the rice and stir to coat with the oil. Add the water, stir, and bring to a boil. Reduce the heat to very low, cover the pot, and cook undisturbed for 18 to 20 minutes, until the rice is soft and has absorbed all the liquid. Remove the lid and fluff with a fork.

3. Combine the peas and rice in a large serving bowl and fold in the red peppers, scallions, chopped thyme, and parsley. Whisk the vinegar, hot sauce, and remaining 4 tablespoons oil in a small bowl, pour over the rice mixture, and stir to combine. Season to taste with salt and pepper and serve warm or at room temperature. *(The salad can be made a few hours in advance, covered, and set aside at room temperature.)*

Serves 8

Grilled Asparagus and Quinoa Salad with Goat Cheese and Spicy Black Olive Vinaigrette

I like to think that bold combinations like olives, honey, and chile powder—three of the seasonings in this lively salad—are what make my food special. You think it sounds like a strange combination? So did I until I tasted it. The big flavors really balance each other out.

This salad has lots of flavor, color, and heft, making it the perfect side for grilled fish or chicken. The goat cheese on top is soft and tangy, but it can be left off if you prefer. Quinoa, a nutty-tasting grain that's a favorite of mine, is easy to buy at whole-foods markets or gourmet stores.

FOR THE VINAIGRETTE:

1 cup pitted Niçoise or other black olives

¼ cup aged sherry vinegar

1 tablespoon Dijon mustard

1 tablespoon honey

1 clove garlic, chopped

½ teaspoon chile de árbol powder (page 10)

½ cup olive oil

Salt and freshly ground black pepper

Combine the olives, vinegar, mustard, honey, garlic, and chile powder in a blender and blend until smooth. With the motor running, slowly add the olive oil and blend until emulsified. Season to taste with salt and pepper. *(The vinaigrette can be made a few hours in advance, covered, and set aside at room temperature.)*

FOR THE SALAD:

2 quarts water

Salt

2 cups quinoa, pearl barley, or long-grain rice

16 spears asparagus, trimmed
Olive oil
Freshly ground black pepper
¼ cup chopped fresh flat-leaf parsley leaves
8 ounces aged goat cheese, thinly sliced

1. Bring the water to a boil in a medium, heavy pot and salt it. Add the quinoa, reduce the heat to very low, cover, and simmer until the quinoa is tender and the water is absorbed, about 20 minutes. Drain if necessary. Transfer to a serving bowl and fluff with a fork. Toss with a few tablespoons of vinaigrette and set aside.

2. Heat your grill to high (page 3).

3. Brush the asparagus with olive oil and season with salt and pepper. Lay the asparagus crosswise on the grate and grill, turning, until charred and just cooked through, 3 to 5 minutes on each side. Remove from the grill and cut into ½-inch pieces.

4. Add the asparagus and parsley to the quinoa and stir to combine. Drizzle some of the vinaigrette over the salad, toss, and season to taste with salt and pepper. Add more vinaigrette if needed. Top with the goat cheese and serve warm or at room temperature. *(The salad can be made a few hours in advance, covered, and set aside at room temperature.)*

Serves 6 to 8

Grilled Potato Salad
with Watercress, Scallions,
and Blue Cheese Vinaigrette

Blue cheese dressing may remind you of the old days, but there's a reason that it's such a classic. With crisp greens, there's nothing better in the world—especially with peppery watercress, which has the crunch to stand up to such an intense dressing. This is a perfect side dish for steak. Make sure to dress the potatoes as soon as they come off the grill; warm potatoes will absorb the dressing and take on the fantastic flavor.

I like the sharp Spanish blue cheese called Cabrales, but you can use whatever blue you like.

16 small new red potatoes (do not peel)
¼ cup aged sherry vinegar,
      or ¼ cup red wine vinegar mixed
      with 2 teaspoons honey
1 small shallot, finely chopped
2 teaspoons Dijon mustard
½ cup olive oil, plus extra for brushing
½ cup crumbled blue cheese
Salt and freshly ground black pepper
8 ounces watercress, coarsely chopped
2 scallions, thinly sliced

1. In a large pot of salted water, boil the potatoes until just cooked through but not soft, 10 to 20 minutes depending on size. Test by piercing a potato with a thin bamboo skewer; when the skewer meets some resistance but can slide all the way through, drain the potatoes immediately. *(The potatoes can be prepared a few hours in advance and set aside; do not refrigerate.)*

2. Whisk the vinegar, shallot, mustard, olive oil, and blue cheese together. *(The vinaigrette can be made a few hours in advance, covered, and kept refrigerated.)*

3. Heat your grill to high (page 3).

4. Cut the potatoes into ¼-inch-thick slices, brush both sides with oil, and sprinkle generously with salt and pepper. Grill until lightly browned on both sides and just cooked through, about 5 minutes total.

5. Arrange the watercress on a platter. Top with the potatoes and scallions. Drizzle the vinaigrette over the top and serve immediately.

Serves 4; can be doubled for 6 to 8

Maple-Glazed Grilled Sweet Potatoes

New York's Latin markets stock an incredible selection of brown, bumpy root vegetables. If you think it's hard to remember the difference between a sweet potato and a yam (what is it again?), try tossing *malanga, batata, name,* and *taro*—all different kinds of sweet potatoes cooked in the Caribbean—into the mix. I haven't found one yet that I didn't like. When cooking any kind of potato on the grill, you want to parboil it first on the stove and grill it after, just to add a little char and smoke.

4 large sweet potatoes (do not peel)
¾ cup pure maple syrup
1 tablespoon ancho chile powder
Salt
¼ cup mild vegetable oil, such as canola

1. Place the potatoes in a large pot and cover with cold water. Bring to a boil over high heat, then reduce the heat and simmer the potatoes until soft but not mushy (you should still feel resistance when you stick a small knife through the center), 25 to 35 minutes.

2. Have ready a bowl of cold water. Drain the potatoes, put them in the cold water, and set aside until cool enough to handle. Peel the potatoes and quarter each one lengthwise. *(The potatoes can be cooked a few hours in advance, covered, and set aside at room temperature. Don't cut them until you're ready to grill.)*

3. Heat your grill to high (page 3).

4. Whisk together the maple syrup, ancho powder, and salt to taste in a small bowl. Brush the potatoes with oil. Grill until golden, about 3 minutes. Brush with the maple glaze and continue grilling, brushing often with the glaze, until the potatoes are glazed, lightly charred, and heated through, about 3 minutes more.

Serves 4

BIG
PARTIES

Fish Taco Party

Ever since I discovered the fish taco, a Cal-Mex specialty that originated around San Diego and Baja, it's been one of my favorite summer dinners, especially for a crowd. The real thing is a soft tortilla wrapped around fried fish, but grilled fish is even better to my taste. With three different fillings—sweet shrimp, flaky snapper, and meaty swordfish—easy homemade garnishes like a slow-cooked tomato salsa and a chunky relish of avocados and tomatillos, and license to eat as much as you want, the only thing missing from your party is the cocktails! (You can eat as much as you want because it's your party—that's my rule!)

For drinks I'd serve Fresh Lemonade with Tequila and Mint Sprigs (page 24), perfect for this casual meal. Make the salsa and the avocado-tomatillo sauce in advance and keep them refrigerated until half an hour before serving. You can also mix the marinades a few hours ahead.

Set up the food on a long table, leaving room for the fish and tortillas when they come off the grill. To make it easy to assemble the tacos, try to follow some sort of logic by keeping the tortillas at one end, the salsas and garnishes at the other, and the platters of fish in the middle, but don't make yourself crazy.

Put the table in a place where people can get to it from both sides, not up against a wall. (And don't put it so close to the grill that you'll be crowded when you're cooking—you're the most important person at the party!) I'm not exactly a decorator, but even I know that a bright tablecloth and a few tea lights in colored glass holders go a long way toward setting a party mood.

Mexican *crema,* a key garnish for the tacos, is slightly soured cream that you can buy at any Mexican grocery store and some supermarkets. *Crema* is not as thick as American sour cream, but you can use sour cream as a substitute. Stir it hard until it turns smooth and runny or thin it with lime juice. Crème fraîche also makes a good substitute.

Smooth Tomato–Serrano Chile Salsa

**2 tablespoons mild vegetable oil,
    such as canola**
1 small red onion, coarsely chopped

4 cloves garlic, coarsely chopped

4 ripe large tomatoes (about 1½ pounds)
    or drained canned tomatoes, chopped

1 serrano chile, stemmed and chopped

¼ cup chopped fresh cilantro leaves

1 tablespoon chopped fresh oregano leaves

3 tablespoons fresh lime juice

Salt and freshly ground black pepper

1. Heat the oil in a medium saucepan over medium-high heat. Add the onion and garlic and cook, stirring, until soft, about 5 minutes; do not let them brown. Add the tomatoes and serrano and cook, stirring, until the tomatoes are soft, 15 to 20 minutes.

2. Transfer the mixture to a blender and blend until smooth. Transfer to a bowl, stir in the cilantro, oregano, and lime juice, and season to taste with salt and pepper. *(The salsa can be made a few hours in advance and kept refrigerated. Bring to room temperature before serving.)*

Grilled Snapper with Citrus Vinaigrette

1½ pounds skinless, flaky white fish fillets,
    such as red snapper or mahimahi

2 tablespoons rice vinegar

2 tablespoons fresh lime juice

2 tablespoons orange juice, preferably fresh

¼ cup mild vegetable oil, such as canola

1 tablespoon ancho chile powder

¼ cup chopped fresh cilantro leaves

Salt and freshly ground black pepper

1. Arrange the fish in a single layer in a large dish. Whisk the vinegar, lime juice, orange juice, oil, ancho powder, and cilantro together, pour over the fish, and marinate for 10 minutes.

2. Heat your grill to high (page 3).

3. Season the fish with salt and pepper. Grill the fish until lightly browned and firm on the bottom, 3 to 4 minutes. Turn the fillets over, reduce the heat to medium or move to a cooler part of the grill, and grill until just cooked through but not falling apart, 2 to 3 minutes more.

4. Remove from the grill and let rest for 5 minutes. Flake the fish with a fork into large chunks, transfer to a bowl, and serve immediately.

Grilled Shrimp with Orange-Cilantro Vinaigrette

24 medium shrimp, shelled and deveined
1 tablespoon grated orange zest
¼ cup fresh orange juice
2 tablespoons finely chopped red onion
1 serrano chile, seeded and chopped
¼ cup fresh cilantro leaves
½ cup mild vegetable oil, such as canola
Salt and freshly ground black pepper
24 wooden skewers, soaked in cold water
      for at least 30 minutes

1. Arrange the shrimp in a single layer in a large dish. Combine the orange zest and juice, onion, chile, and cilantro in a blender and blend until smooth. With the motor running, slowly pour in the oil and blend until emulsified. Season to taste with salt and pepper, pour over the shrimp, and marinate for 10 minutes.

2. Heat your grill to high (page 3).

3. Spear the shrimp by pushing the skewer through the head and the tail, then smoothing the shrimp along the skewer to help it lie flat. Season the shrimp with salt and pepper. Grill the shrimp until pink, opaque, and just cooked through, 1½ to 2 minutes on each side. Transfer to a platter and serve immediately.

Grilled Swordfish
with Lime-Basil-Jalapeño Vinaigrette

1½ pounds swordfish steak, 1 inch thick
Grated zest of 1 lime
¼ cup fresh lime juice
2 jalapeño chiles, seeded and chopped
¼ cup packed fresh basil leaves
½ cup mild vegetable oil, such as canola
Salt and freshly ground pepper

1. Place the fish in a large dish. Combine the lime zest and juice, chiles, and basil in a blender and blend until smooth. With the motor running, slowly pour in the oil and blend until emulsified. Season to taste with salt and pepper, pour over the fish, turn to coat, and marinate for 10 minutes.

2. Heat your grill to high (page 3).

3. Grill the fish until lightly browned and firm on the bottom, 3 to 4 minutes. Turn the fish over, reduce the heat to medium or move to a cooler part of the grill, and grill until just cooked through (page 5), 3 to 4 minutes more. Remove the fish from the grill and slice ½ inch thick. Transfer to a platter and serve immediately.

FOR THE TACOS:
Avocado-Tomatillo Sauce (page 152)
½ head iceberg lettuce, thinly shredded
½ head red cabbage, cored and thinly
   shredded
Thinly sliced red onions
Thinly sliced scallions
Chopped fresh cilantro leaves
Hot sauce
Mexican *crema* (see headnote)
6-inch tortillas, flour and/or corn
   (plan on at least 3 tacos per person)

1. Put all the taco garnishes and sauces in colorful bowls and plates and arrange them on a table.

2. Heat your grill to high (page 3).

3. Place the tortillas on the grill and grill for 20 seconds on each side, just until warm and lightly charred. Serve in baskets lined with cloth napkins or kitchen towels to keep them warm.

Serves 8

Burger Bar

Burgers are one of life's great pleasures. Seriously. They're easy, juicy, simple, and totally satisfying. I bet your friends think so too. Serve the burgers with Pineapple-Mint Tequila Fizz (page 23); it will be the best burger and soda they've ever had!

The toppings can be prepared beforehand and, of course, there's no need to serve all of them—these are just suggestions. If you have a big table, just put all the toppings in the center; if not, set up a separate toppings bar to prevent traffic jams.

The thing I won't compromise on is the buns: They have to be soft, not crusty, so they can soak up the delicious juices.

You can make the burgers in advance (except for cooking them, of course). Keep them refrigerated until about 15 minutes before grilling. Plan on two burgers per person.

Chipotle Ketchup

1 cup ketchup
1 tablespoon chipotle purée (page 12)

Combine the ingredients in a small bowl. *(The ketchup can be made a few days in advance, covered, and kept refrigerated. Bring to room temperature before serving.)*

Green Chile Mayonnaise

1 cup mayonnaise
1 poblano chile, roasted, peeled, seeded,
    and coarsely chopped (page 9)
2 tablespoons chopped red onion
2 cloves garlic, chopped
1 tablespoon mild vegetable oil, such as canola
1 tablespoon honey
Juice of 1 lime
Salt and freshly ground black pepper

Combine all the ingredients in a blender and blend until smooth. Scrape into a bowl and refrigerate for at least 1 hour before serving. *(The mayonnaise can be made a few days in advance, covered, and kept refrigerated. Serve cold.)*

Guacamole

5 ripe Hass avocados, halved, pitted, peeled,
  and diced
½ small red onion, finely chopped
1 serrano chile, seeded and minced
¼ cup chopped fresh cilantro leaves
Juice of 1 lime
2 tablespoons mild vegetable oil,
  such as canola
Salt and freshly ground black pepper

Combine all the ingredients in a medium bowl and season to taste with salt and pepper. *(The guacamole can be made a few hours in advance, covered, and kept refrigerated.)*

Salsa Fresca

3 ripe beefsteak tomatoes, diced
½ red onion, chopped
1 jalapeño chile, seeded and minced
3 tablespoons olive oil
Juice of 1 lime
3 tablespoons chopped fresh cilantro leaves
Salt and freshly ground black pepper

Combine all the ingredients in a medium bowl and season to taste with salt and pepper. Let sit at room temperature for 30 minutes. *(The salsa can be made a few hours in advance, covered, and kept refrigerated.)*

The Best Burgers

FOR THE TOPPINGS:

Mustard (I like horseradish mustard
    for burgers)
Thickly sliced Cheddar, American,
    and/or Brie cheeses
Crumbled blue and/or goat cheeses
Watercress
Romaine and Boston lettuce leaves

Set up your toppings bar (see headnote), arranging the mustard, ketchup, mayonnaise, guacamole, and salsa in bowls, and the cheeses, watercress, and lettuces on platters.

FOR THE BURGERS:

2 large sweet onions,
    such as Vidalia or Walla Walla,
    sliced ½ inch thick
Mild vegetable oil, such as canola
3 pounds ground beef chuck,
    80% lean, formed into 6-ounce
    burgers
Salt and freshly ground black pepper
3 pounds ground turkey,
    formed into 6-ounce burgers
3 pounds ground buffalo,
    formed into 6-ounce burgers
24 soft sesame seed buns

1. Heat your grill to high (page 3).

2. Brush the onion slices with oil. Grill until softened and lightly charred, about 5 minutes on each side. Transfer to a plate and add to the toppings bar. Leave the grill on.

3. Season each beef burger with salt and pepper. Grill until crusty, browned, and lightly

charred, 4 to 5 minutes. Turn the burgers over and grill until medium-rare (page 5), about 2 minutes more.

4. Brush the turkey burgers with oil and season with salt and pepper. Grill until crusty, browned, and lightly charred, 4 to 5 minutes. Turn the burgers over and grill until just cooked through (page 5), 3 to 4 minutes more.

5. Brush the buffalo burgers with oil and season with salt and pepper. Grill until crusty, browned, and lightly charred, 4 to 5 minutes. Turn the burgers over and grill until medium-rare (page 5), about 2 minutes more.

6. As you cook the burgers, use the cooler parts of the grill to toast the buns for 1 to 2 minutes on the cut sides. Serve immediately.

Serves 12

Skewer Party

This is a great idea for a party when you want your guests to be able to wander around, stay clean, and look cool. Burgers and tacos are a two-hand operation, but skewers can be eaten with one. You can put a cocktail glass in your guest's other hand! The recipes—lamb, chicken, shrimp, pork, and beef—are seasoned completely differently; they are similar enough to work together but not enough to be boring.

Grill each kind of skewer separately. Don't try to grill a few chicken, a few shrimp, and a few beef at the same time, or you'll go nuts trying to get them off the grill at the right moment. To serve, ask a couple of guests to carry platters of skewers around the party. Nothing formal, but since each skewer is just a couple of bites, you don't want your guests hovering around the grill looking for more!

You can mix and match the recipes to suit the season and your tastes, and there are other skewered dishes elsewhere in this book that you can add (pages 90, 101, 110, 116, and 170). You'll want to have a total of about 6 to 8 ounces of meat per person, depending on what else you're serving. I'd recommend Grilled Flatbread with Cucumber-Yogurt Salad and Toasted Walnuts (page 38) and Tomato Bread (page 37) to start. If you want to do the whole party as finger food, add your favorite vegetables—baby carrots, endive spears, radishes—and a couple of dips from pages 26 to 34.

Lamb Tenderloin with Serrano-Mint Glaze

2 cups red wine vinegar

2 cups white wine vinegar

2 cups sugar

2 serrano chiles, chopped

1 cup fresh mint leaves

2 (1-pound) lamb tenderloins, or 2 pounds
    lamb loin cut into 1-inch pieces

6-inch wooden skewers, soaked
    in cold water for at least 30 minutes

Olive oil

Salt and freshly ground black pepper

1. Combine the vinegars and sugar in a medium saucepan (not aluminum or cast-iron) and bring to a boil. Boil until reduced to 1 cup. Let cool slightly, transfer to a blender, add the serrano chiles and mint, and process until smooth. Pour into a bowl. *(The glaze can be made a few days in advance, covered, and kept refrigerated. Bring to room temperature before using.)*

2. Heat your grill to high (page 3). Set aside a few tablespoons of the glaze to use after the cooking.

3. Spear 3 pieces of lamb onto each skewer, keeping them together at one end of the skewer (this will make the skewer easier to hold). Brush the lamb on both sides with oil and season with salt and pepper.

4. Grill the lamb, brushing with the glaze every minute or so, until medium-rare (page 5), 2 to 3 minutes on both sides.

5. Remove to a platter and brush with the reserved glaze. Let rest for 2 minutes before serving.

Tandoori Chicken

FOR THE MARINADE:

1 cup thick yogurt (page 12)

1 small yellow onion, coarsely chopped

4 cloves garlic, coarsely chopped

1 (1-inch) piece fresh ginger, peeled
   and coarsely chopped

½ teaspoon saffron threads mixed
   with ¼ cup warm water

1 teaspoon grated lime zest

¼ cup fresh lime juice

2 teaspoons salt

2 teaspoons ground coriander

1 teaspoon ground cumin

1 teaspoon cayenne

1 teaspoon turmeric

½ teaspoon ground white pepper

Combine the ingredients for the marinade in a baking dish or sealable plastic bag and mix well.

FOR THE CHICKEN:

4 large boneless, skinless chicken breast halves (about 2 pounds), cut into 1-inch pieces

6-inch wooden skewers, soaked in cold water for at least 30 minutes

Salt and freshly ground black pepper

---

1. Add the chicken to the marinade and turn to coat. Cover and refrigerate for at least 4 hours and up to 8 hours.

2. Heat your grill to high (page 3).

3. Spear 3 pieces of chicken onto each skewer, keeping them together at one end of the skewer (this will make the skewer easier to hold) and season with salt and pepper.

4. Grill the chicken until golden brown and just cooked through (page 5), about 3 minutes on each side. Serve immediately.

Lime-Cilantro-Glazed Shrimp

---

2 cups fresh lime juice

1 cup red wine vinegar

2 cups sugar

1 cup packed fresh cilantro leaves, plus extra for garnish

Salt and freshly ground black pepper

16 medium shrimp, peeled and deveined

6-inch wooden skewers, soaked in cold water for at least 30 minutes

Olive oil

---

1. Combine the lime juice, vinegar, and sugar in a medium saucepan (not aluminum or cast-iron) and bring to a boil. Boil until reduced to 1 cup. Let cool slightly, transfer to a

blender, add the cilantro, and blend until smooth. Season to taste with salt and pepper. *(The glaze can be made a few days in advance, covered, and kept refrigerated. Bring to room temperature before serving.)*

2. Heat your grill to high (page 3). Set aside a few tablespoons of the glaze to use after the cooking.

3. Spear one shrimp onto each skewer, pushing the skewer through both ends of the shrimp to help it lie flat on the grill. Brush the shrimp with oil and season with salt and pepper.

4. Grill the shrimp, brushing often with the glaze, until pink, opaque, and just cooked through, 1½ to 2 minutes on each side. Remove the shrimp to a platter and brush with the reserved glaze. Sprinkle with cilantro and serve immediately.

Pork with Molasses-Mustard Glaze

¼ **cup molasses (not blackstrap)**
½ **cup Dijon mustard**
Salt and freshly ground black pepper
1½ **pounds pork tenderloin,**
    cut into 1-inch pieces
6-inch wooden skewers, soaked in cold water
    for at least 30 minutes
Olive oil

1. Whisk together the molasses and mustard in a bowl and season with salt and pepper.

2. Heat your grill to high (page 3). Set aside a few tablespoons of the glaze to use after the cooking.

3. Spear 3 pieces of pork onto each skewer, keeping them together at one end of the skewer (this will make the skewer easier to hold). Brush the pork with oil and season with salt and pepper.

4. Grill the pork, brushing often with the glaze, until just cooked through (page 5), 3 to 4 minutes on each side. Remove to a platter and brush with the reserved glaze. Serve immediately.

Hoisin-Glazed Beef

2 tablespoons peanut oil

4 cloves garlic, finely chopped

1 (2-inch) piece fresh ginger,
   peeled and finely chopped

½ cup hoisin sauce

1 tablespoon honey

Salt and freshly ground black pepper

1½ pounds beef tenderloin,
   cut into 1-inch pieces

6-inch wooden skewers, soaked
   in cold water for at least 30 minutes

Olive oil

1. Heat the peanut oil in a saucepan over medium-high heat. Add the garlic and ginger and cook, stirring, until soft, about 2 minutes; do not brown. Remove the pan from the heat, stir in the hoisin and honey, and season to taste with salt and pepper. *(The glaze can be made a few days in advance, covered, and kept refrigerated. Bring to room temperature before serving.)*

2. Heat your grill to high (page 3). Set aside a few tablespoons of the glaze to use after the cooking.

3. Spear 3 pieces of beef onto each skewer, keeping them together at one end of the skewer (this will make the skewer easier to hold). Brush the meat on both sides with olive oil and season with salt and pepper.

4. Grill the beef, brushing often with the glaze, until medium-rare (page 5), 2 to 3 minutes on each side. Remove to a platter and brush with the reserved glaze. Serve immediately.

Serves 10 to 12

FISH AND SHELLFISH

Grilled Clams in the Shell
with Serrano Ham

Clams and ham (or bacon in the case of clam chowder) are a bit of an odd couple. You wouldn't think they'd go together, but the combination of two salty ingredients is actually perfect. In Portugal and Spain, they're often combined in a single dish. I love grilled clams; they're fun to make, totally easy, and impressive. Show off a little by dumping the clams all at once onto the grate of the grill. It makes a serious clatter!

This dish makes a great tapa, a little appetizer designed to serve with wine as your guests arrive. Serrano ham, my personal favorite, is like a Spanish prosciutto. Serve it alongside Tomato Bread (page 37; leave out the prosciutto in that recipe).

32 littleneck clams, scrubbed

4 slices serrano ham, torn into small pieces
   (about 32 pieces total)

Extra-virgin olive oil

Hot sauce

1. Heat your grill to high (page 3).

2. Place the clams directly on the grate of the grill, close the cover, and cook until the clams open, 5 to 7 minutes (discard any clams that do not open).

3. Remove the clams to a platter, stuff each one with a piece of ham, and drizzle the whole platter with olive oil. Immediately serve the clams in the shell with a dash of hot sauce in each clam.

Serves 4 as an appetizer; can be doubled for 6 to 8

Grilled Sea Scallops
with Papaya-Tomatillo Salsa

This is a Mesa Grill classic, one of those dishes that my customers won't let me take off the menu. Now my secret is out—scallops are really, really easy to grill. As long as you make sure to brush them all over with oil and don't overcook them, scallops will not let you down. They cook evenly and quickly and develop a nice golden brown crust.

If possible, buy your scallops from a good fish market with high turnover; they will be fresh and pure. (Some supermarket scallops are treated with whiteners and weighted with extra water.)

FOR THE SALSA:

**2 ripe papayas, peeled, seeded,
    and coarsely chopped**
**6 tomatillos, husked, washed,
    and coarsely chopped**
½ red onion, finely diced
2 jalapeño chiles, finely diced
¼ cup chopped fresh cilantro leaves
¼ cup fresh lime juice
**2 tablespoons mild vegetable oil,
    such as canola**
1 tablespoon honey
Salt and freshly ground black pepper

Combine all the ingredients in a serving bowl and season to taste with salt and pepper. Let sit at room temperature for at least 30 minutes. *(The salsa can be made a few hours in advance, covered, and kept refrigerated. Bring to room temperature before serving.)*

FOR THE SCALLOPS:

20 large sea scallops, muscle removed

Mild vegetable oil, such as canola

Salt and freshly ground black pepper

1. Heat your grill to high (page 3).

2. Brush the scallops on both sides with oil, making sure they are well coated, and season with salt and pepper. Grill until crusty, golden brown, and just cooked through (page 5), 2 to 3 minutes on each side. Remove to a platter or serving plates and spoon the salsa on top. Serve immediately.

Serves 4; can be doubled for 6 to 8

Barbecued Brisket Sandwiches
on Texas Toast (page 210) and
Grilled Corn on the Cob
with Garlic Butter, Fresh Lime,
and Queso Fresco (page 70)

Clockwise from right: Smoky Red Pepper and White Bean Dip (page 34); Grilled Flatbread with Cucumber-Yogurt Salad and Toasted Walnuts (page 38); Feta and Scallion Dip with Olive Oil and Lemon (page 30); and Rosé Sangria (page 20)

Grilled Tuna with Red Chile, Allspice, and Orange Glaze (page 150)

Pressed Cuban-Style Burger (page 198) and Mojitos (page 21)

Grilled Quesadillas with Sliced Steak,
Blue Cheese, and Watercress (page 46)

Thick-Cut Ribeye with Red Wine–Honey Mustard Vinaigrette and Fresh Thyme (page 218) and Grilled Potato Salad with Watercress, Scallions, and Blue Cheese Vinaigrette (page 84)

Jerk-Rubbed Chicken Thighs
with Homemade Habanero
Hot Sauce (page 168)

Beer-Simmered Bratwurst with Grilled Onions and Red Sauerkraut (page 240)

Thin Pork Chops with
Fresh Nectarine-Ginger
Chutney (page 236)

Porterhouse Steaks with Fra Diavolo Barbecue Sauce and Cherry Pepper Salad (page 206)

Cedar-Planked Lobster Tails with Corn and Smoked Chile Relish (page 128)

**Maple-Peach-Glazed
Ham Steak (page 239)
with scrambled eggs**

Grilled Bacon, Lettuce, Green Tomato, and Goat Cheese Sandwich (page 238)

Skewer Party (page 97):
Lime-Cilantro-Glazed
Shrimp (page 99),
Hoisin-Glazed Beef
(page 101), Tandoori
Chicken (page 98),
and Pork with Molasses-
Mustard Glaze (page 100)

Fish
Taco Party
(page 88), clockwise from
left: Avocado-Tomatillo Sauce
(page 162); Smooth Tomato-Serrano
Chile Salsa (page 88); Mexican crema;
Grilled Shrimp with Orange-Cilantro
Vinaigrette (page 90); hot sauce; Grilled
Swordfish with Lime-Basil-Jalapeño
Vinaigrette (page 91); sliced red
cabbage, red onion, iceberg
lettuce, and scallions;
and grilled tortillas.

Grilled Pineapple with Butter-Rum Glaze
and Vanilla Mascarpone (page 248)

Grilled Sea Scallop Salad
with Endive and Arugula

Rich scallops and bitter greens are a fabulous combination that makes a perfect first course, or a summer lunch with bread, cheese, and ripe figs or peaches. The crunch of the endive is especially good with soft scallops.

1 head Belgian endive, thinly sliced crosswise
2 cups baby arugula leaves, or regular arugula
    torn into small pieces
12 large sea scallops, muscle removed
Olive oil
Salt and freshly ground black pepper
Spicy Black Olive Vinaigrette (page 82)

1. Heat your grill to high (page 3).

2. Divide the endive and arugula among 4 serving plates. Brush the scallops on both sides with oil, making sure they are well coated, and season with salt and pepper.

3. Grill the scallops until crusty, golden brown, and just cooked through, 2 to 3 minutes on each side. Divide the scallops on top of the greens, spoon a little vinaigrette over, and serve immediately.

Serves 4 as an appetizer; can be doubled for 6 to 8 (no need to double the dressing)

Grilled Shrimp Taquitos with Asparagus, Red Cabbage, and Creamy Chipotle Sauce

My weakness in sushi restaurants isn't just the incredibly fresh fish but also the delicious spicy mayonnaise that the fish is sometimes wrapped with. I love the combination of creamy and sharp, so I created a similar sauce for shrimp and asparagus that I am completely addicted to. Make sure not to overcook the asparagus; you want them to keep a bit of crunch. Wrap it all up together in a warm tortilla. I like to cut the tortillas into a miniature, two-bite size with a biscuit cutter, but you can use 6-inch tortillas if you prefer.

FOR THE SAUCE:

1 cup mayonnaise

2 tablespoons chipotle purée (page 12)

Salt and freshly ground black pepper

Fresh lime juice

Whisk together the mayonnaise and chipotle purée in a small bowl and season with salt, pepper, and lime juice to taste. *(The sauce can be made a few hours in advance, covered, and kept refrigerated.)*

FOR THE CABBAGE:

½ cup mild vegetable oil, such as canola

½ cup fresh orange juice

¼ cup fresh lime juice

½ small red onion, coarsely chopped

2 cloves garlic, finely chopped

¼ cup fresh basil leaves

2 tablespoons chopped fresh cilantro leaves

1 tablespoon honey

Salt and freshly ground black pepper

½ head red cabbage, cored and finely shredded

Combine all the ingredients except the cabbage in a blender and blend until smooth. Season to taste with salt and pepper. Place the cabbage in a large bowl and toss with the vinaigrette. Taste for salt and pepper and refrigerate for at least 30 minutes before serving. *(The cabbage can be made 2 hours in advance, covered, and kept refrigerated.)*

FOR THE TACOS:

16 large shrimp, peeled and deveined

16 small wooden skewers, soaked
    in cold water for at least 30 minutes

Olive oil

Salt and freshly ground black pepper

16 thin stalks asparagus, trimmed

16 to 24 flour tortillas, depending
    on size (see headnote)

Fresh cilantro leaves

1. Heat your grill to high (page 3).

2. Spear one shrimp onto each skewer, pushing the skewer through both ends of the shrimp to help it lie flat on the grill. Brush the shrimp with oil and season with salt and pepper. Grill the shrimp until pink, opaque, and just cooked through, 1½ to 2 minutes on each side.

3. Brush the asparagus with oil and season with salt and pepper. Lay the asparagus across the grate of the grill and grill until browned and just cooked through, 2 to 3 minutes on each side. Remove from the grill and cut the asparagus crosswise in half.

4. Grill the tortillas just until warmed and flexible, about 20 seconds on each side.

5. Assemble the tacos: Fold 1 shrimp, 2 pieces of asparagus, some cabbage, chipotle mayonnaise, and cilantro leaves into each tortilla. Serve immediately.

Serves 4; can be doubled for 6 to 8 (no need to double the dressing or the slaw)

Grilled Shrimp
with Triple Lemon Butter

BOBBY
FLAY'S
BOY
GETS
GRILL

112

Cooking just doesn't get quicker than this. It's become my go-to recipe when it's 4 P.M. and I suddenly realize that I've invited ten people to dinner! During the summer, I keep a few flavored butters on hand in the freezer for situations like this. It really pays off, because it means I've always got a sauce on hand. Add a tomato salad and rice, and you're done.

I worked overtime getting this butter just right. It's extra lemony, packed with lemon essence and perfume, but not extra sour. Simmering down the lemon juice is the key. To make lemon-basil butter, another favorite of mine, add 12 large basil leaves to the food processor.

FOR THE BUTTER:

6 to 10 lemons, depending on size

8 tablespoons (1 stick) unsalted butter, slightly softened

½ teaspoon salt

½ teaspoon coarsely ground black pepper

1. Set one lemon aside for step 2. Squeeze the juice from the remaining lemons until you have 1½ cups. Place the lemon juice in a small saucepan (not aluminum or cast-iron) and boil until syrupy and reduced to ¼ cup. Let cool.

2. Grate the zest from the reserved lemon and set the zest aside. Using a small knife, cut off all the white pith to expose the yellow flesh of the lemon. Chop the lemon flesh, discarding the pits and membranes.

3. Combine the butter, lemon zest, chopped lemon, cooled lemon syrup, and the salt and pepper in a food processor or electric mixer and process until smooth. (To mix by hand, let the butter get very soft, then beat all the ingredients together with a large wooden spoon.) *(The butter can be made in advance, covered, and kept refrigerated for a few days, or frozen for a week. Bring to room temperature before serving.)*

FOR THE SHRIMP:

20 extra-large shrimp, peeled and deveined

Olive oil

Salt and freshly ground black pepper

2 tablespoons finely chopped fresh chives

1. Heat your grill to high (page 3).

2. Brush the shrimp with oil and season with salt and pepper. Grill the shrimp until pink, opaque, and just cooked through, 1½ to 2 minutes on each side. Remove the shrimp to a platter and brush the hot shrimp with lemon butter. Sprinkle with chives and serve immediately.

Serves 4; can be doubled for 6 to 8 (no need to double the butter)

Rum–Brown Sugar–Glazed Shrimp
with Lime and Cilantro

BOBBY
FLAY'S
BOY
GETS
GRILL

114

Rum and brown sugar are both made from sugarcane, so they make a natural combination—and a great glaze for shrimp. The spice in the rum and the freshness of lime balance the sweetness. When you're looking for a fast, fresh shrimp dish, this is it. Serve with grilled corn on the cob (page 70) and avocado salad (page 56) for a quick, fun summer dinner.

FOR THE GLAZE:

1 cup dark rum

¾ cup light brown sugar

1 teaspoon coarsely ground black pepper

Pinch of salt

Combine the rum and brown sugar in a small saucepan and simmer until the sugar is completely dissolved and the mixture is reduced by half. Add the pepper and season to taste with salt. *(The glaze can be made a few days in advance, covered, and kept refrigerated. Bring to room temperature before serving.)*

FOR THE SHRIMP:

24 large shrimp, peeled and deveined

Olive oil

Salt and freshly ground black pepper

2 limes, zest grated and quartered

3 tablespoons chopped fresh cilantro leaves

1. Heat your grill to high (page 3). Set aside a few tablespoons of glaze for brushing the cooked shrimp.

2. Brush the shrimp with oil and season with salt and pepper to taste. Grill the shrimp, brushing often with the glaze, until pink, opaque, and just cooked through, 1½ to 2 min-

utes on each side. Remove to a platter and brush with the reserved glaze. Squeeze the lime quarters over the shrimp and sprinkle with lime zest and chopped cilantro. Serve immediately.

Serves 4; can be doubled for 6 to 8 (no need to double the glaze)

Grilled Shrimp Skewers
with Soy Sauce, Fresh Ginger,
and Toasted Sesame Seeds

BOBBY
FLAY'S
BOY
GETS
GRILL

116

Sometimes you develop a craving for a dish that doesn't exist, so you have to invent it yourself. I love the classic Chinese seasonings of soy, ginger, sesame oil, and chile, and I wanted to eat them with one of my favorites—fat, sweet shrimp lightly charred on the grill. It turns out that this is not a dish you can order at a Chinese restaurant (believe me, I tried!), so I made it at home. Serve on top of white rice with a side of Crunchy Vegetable Slaw with Peanut Sauce and Crispy Noodles (page 66).

**24 medium or large shrimp, shelled
and deveined**

**24 small wooden skewers, soaked in water
for at least 30 minutes**

⅓ cup soy sauce

2 cloves garlic, finely chopped

1 tablespoon grated fresh ginger

1 tablespoon toasted sesame oil

1 tablespoon fresh lime juice

½ teaspoon hot red pepper flakes

**2 tablespoons sesame seeds, toasted
(page 10)**

**2 scallions, white and pale green parts only,
thinly sliced on the diagonal**

1. Spear the shrimp by pushing a skewer through the head and the tail, then smoothing the shrimp along the skewer to help it lie flat.

2. Whisk the soy sauce, garlic, ginger, sesame oil, lime juice, and pepper flakes in a small bowl. Place the shrimp skewers in a single layer in a large dish, pour the marinade over them, and turn to coat. Cover and let marinate in the refrigerator for 1 hour, turning once.

3. Heat your grill to high (page 3).

4. Grill the shrimp until pink, opaque, and just cooked through, 1½ to 2 minutes on each side. Remove to a platter and sprinkle with sesame seeds and scallions. Serve immediately.

Serves 4; can be doubled for 6 to 8

Fire-Roasted Prawns
with Habanero-Garlic Vinaigrette

BOBBY
FLAY'S
BOY
GETS
GRILL

118

This is a dig-in-and-get-your-hands-dirty kind of dish—fun and flavorful. Cooking the sweet prawns in the shells keeps them juicy; drizzling them while they're still hot with a spicy, garlicky, lime juice–spiked vinaigrette makes them irresistible. Serve as a first course or as part of a Caribbean menu alongside Grilled Halibut with Mango, Serrano, and Scallion Relish (page 140).

FOR THE VINAIGRETTE:
6 cloves garlic, peeled and left whole
¾ cup olive oil
½ fresh habanero or Scotch bonnet chile, seeded and chopped
¼ cup fresh lime juice
2 tablespoons water
1 tablespoon honey
¼ cup chopped fresh cilantro leaves
Salt and freshly ground black pepper

1. Combine the garlic and olive oil in a small saucepan, place over low heat, and simmer gently until the garlic turns light golden, about 8 minutes. Let cool slightly.

2. Lift the garlic cloves out of the oil and place in a blender; set the oil aside. Add the chile, lime juice, water, and honey to the garlic and blend until smooth. With the motor running, slowly add ½ cup of the garlic-infused oil and blend until emulsified. Add the cilantro and blend for 5 seconds. Season to taste with salt and pepper. *(The vinaigrette can be made a few hours in advance, covered, and kept refrigerated. Bring to room temperature and whisk or shake well before serving.)*

FOR THE PRAWNS:

16 large prawns (jumbo shrimp), in the shell
Salt and freshly ground black pepper
Chopped fresh cilantro leaves

1. Heat your grill to high (page 3).

2. Brush the prawns with the remaining garlic oil and season with salt and pepper. Grill the prawns until pink, opaque, and just cooked through, 2 minutes on each side. Remove the prawns to a platter. Immediately drizzle with the vinaigrette and shower with chopped cilantro. Serve at once.

Serves 4; can be doubled for 6 to 8 (no need to double the dressing)

Grilled Soft-Shell Crab Sandwich with Smoked Chile Tartar Sauce

BOBBY
FLAY'S
BOY
GETS
GRILL

120

I've stuffed two of my favorite sandwiches—the soft-shell crab and the BLT—into one bun. The spicy, creamy sauce has all the smokiness of bacon (from the smoked chipotle chiles), the crunch and sourness of tartar sauce, and the irresistible texture of mayonnaise. On top of a lightly charred soft-shell, with a slice of summer's ripest beefsteak and a few peppery arugula leaves, there's nothing better.

This recipe serves four normal people or two big-time soft-shell crab fans. You may have extra tartar sauce, but leftovers get used up very quickly at my house! Try it instead of mayo on your favorite sandwich.

FOR THE SAUCE:

½ **cup mayonnaise**

1 **teaspoon chipotle purée (page 12),
or more to taste**

1 **teaspoon fresh lime juice**

1 **clove garlic, finely chopped**

2 **sweet gherkins, finely diced**

1 **teaspoon capers, drained (chop if large)**

2 **tablespoons chopped fresh cilantro leaves**

Salt and freshly ground black pepper

Combine all the ingredients in a medium bowl and season with salt and pepper to taste. Cover and refrigerate for at least 1 hour before serving. *(The sauce can be made a day in advance, covered, and kept refrigerated.)*

FOR THE SANDWICHES:

4 **soft-shell crabs (buy them cleaned
or have someone at the fish counter
clean them for you)**

Olive oil

Salt and freshly ground black pepper

4 seeded hamburger buns

Arugula leaves

8 slices ripe beefsteak tomato

½ red onion, thinly sliced

1. Heat your grill to high (page 3).

2. Brush the crabs with oil and season with salt and pepper. Grill the crabs until the legs are completely pink (no longer blue), 3 to 4 minutes on each side.

3. Spread tartar sauce on the buns. Put arugula, tomato, and onion on the bottom half of each bun. Top with the crabs, then the bun tops, press lightly, and serve immediately.

Serves 4; can be doubled for 6 to 8

Grilled Split Lobsters with Curry Butter

BOBBY
FLAY'S
BOY
GETS
GRILL

122

When I slather hot lobsters with this aromatic spiced butter, the incredible perfume that rises takes me right back to the Caribbean. Sitting on the beach with a glass of rum-spiked lemonade on an island near Anguilla, I had my first taste of the local grilled lobsters. Since then, adding smokiness to the sweet, briny flavors of lobster has become one of my favorite projects on the grill.

The curry butter might seem out of place, but actually Anguilla is one of many Caribbean islands where the food has a lot of Indian flavor. The spices of Indian cooking have mixed with local ingredients to create aromatic dishes like this one.

FOR THE BUTTER:
2 tablespoons olive oil
½ small red onion, finely chopped
3 cloves garlic, finely chopped
3 tablespoons good-quality curry powder
2 cups white wine
8 ounces (2 sticks) unsalted butter,
    slightly softened
Salt

1. Heat the oil in a small saucepan over medium-high heat. Add the onion and garlic and cook, stirring, until soft, about 5 minutes; do not brown. Add the curry powder and cook, stirring, for 3 minutes. Add the wine and simmer until reduced to about ¼ cup, 10 to 12 minutes. Set aside to cool.

2. Place the butter in a bowl, add the curry mixture, and mix well. Season to taste with salt. Cover and refrigerate until cold, about 2 hours. *(The butter can be made in advance, covered, and kept refrigerated a few days, or frozen for a week. Bring to room temperature before serving.)*

FOR THE LOBSTER:

4 (1½-pound) live lobsters

Olive oil

Salt and freshly ground black pepper

¼ cup chopped fresh cilantro leaves

1. In a large pot of boiling salted water, parboil the lobsters for 12 to 15 minutes (they will be about three-quarters done). Let cool. *(The lobsters can be parboiled a few hours in advance, covered, and kept refrigerated. Bring to room temperature before proceeding.)*

2. Heat your grill to high (page 3).

3. Split each lobster down the front (the underside) with a heavy knife, taking care not to cut through the back shell, so that the lobster is still in one piece but the inside is exposed. Brush the cut sides of the lobsters with oil and season with salt and pepper.

4. Place the lobsters cut side up on the grill and cook until lightly charred and heated through, 5 to 7 minutes. Remove from the grill and brush with plenty of butter. Shower with chopped cilantro and serve immediately.

Serves 4; can be doubled for 8 (no need to double the butter)

Grilled Lobster Rolls
with Scallion Mayonnaise

BOBBY
FLAY'S
BOY
GETS
GRILL

124

Lobster rolls—chunks of lobster mixed with mayo and served on a hot dog bun—are the perfect summer lunch. Boiled or steamed lobster is the usual choice, but I like to put a light char on the lobster before taking it out of the shell. The results are sweet and smoky, perfect with this fresh-tasting mayonnaise. Serve with grilled corn on the cob, and don't forget to grill the buns—you definitely want that toasty crispness.

FOR THE MAYONNAISE:
10 scallions, green parts only, coarsely chopped
1 cup mayonnaise
2 cloves garlic, chopped
1 tablespoon grated lemon zest
Salt and freshly ground black pepper

Place the scallions in a food processor or blender and process until finely chopped. Add the mayonnaise, garlic, and lemon zest and process until combined. (To do this by hand, finely chop the scallions and garlic and mix in the other ingredients with a spoon.) Season to taste with salt and pepper. Cover and refrigerate for at least 1 hour. (*The mayonnaise can be made a day in advance, covered, and kept refrigerated.*)

FOR THE LOBSTER ROLLS:
4 (2½-pound) live lobsters (to yield 2 pounds
     cooked lobster meat)
Mild vegetable oil, such as canola
Salt and freshly ground black pepper
2 small ribs celery, sliced ¼ inch thick
¼ cup finely chopped red onion
¼ cup chopped fresh cilantro leaves
8 split-top hot dog buns
Olive oil

1. In a large pot of boiling salted water, parboil the lobsters for 12 to 15 minutes (they will be about three-quarters done). Let cool. (*The lobsters can be parboiled a few hours in advance, covered, and kept refrigerated. Bring to room temperature before proceeding.*)

2. Heat your grill to high (page 3).

3. Split each lobster down the front (the underside) with a heavy knife, taking care not to cut through the back shell, so that the lobster is still in one piece but the inside is exposed. Brush the cut sides of the lobsters with vegetable oil and season with salt and pepper.

4. Place the lobsters cut side up on the grill and cook until lightly charred and heated through, 5 to 7 minutes. Set aside and reduce the grill heat to medium.

5. When the lobsters are cool enough to handle, remove the meat from the shells and cut into bite-size chunks. Place the meat in a large bowl and add the celery, onion, cilantro, and half of the scallion mayonnaise. Mix, adding more of the mayonnaise if needed to bind the mixture. Season to taste with salt and pepper.

6. Brush the tops and insides of the rolls with olive oil. Grill split side down until golden, 30 to 45 seconds. Divide the lobster salad among the buns and serve immediately.

Serves 4

Cedar-Planked Lobster Tails with Corn and Smoked Chile Relish

Sometimes—admit it—part of the fun of grilling is showing off. When you're doing something really cool, like smoking lobster tails between two planks of wood, it's fun to have an audience to appreciate it. More important, the results taste amazing. The smoky, piney cedar perfumes the sweet lobster like you would not believe. This method was traditionally used by the Native Americans of the Pacific Northwest to cook salmon, and it still works.

You'll need untreated cedar planks, which you can buy at a lumberyard or at *www.barbecuewood.com* or *www.justsmokedsalmon.com*. For the freshest lobster tails, the Internet is also your best bet: Visit *www.mainelobsterdirect.com* or *www.thelobster-net.com*. You can also buy lobster tails at the fish counter or make your own by parboiling lobsters as described on page 123 and removing the tails. Use the claw meat to make lobster rolls (page 124) for lunch the next day.

FOR THE RELISH:

8 ears corn, silks removed, husks left on, soaked in cold water for 10 minutes

½ red onion, thinly sliced

2 teaspoons chipotle purée (page 12)

¼ cup fresh lime juice

3 tablespoons mild vegetable oil, such as canola

2 tablespoons chopped fresh cilantro leaves

2 tablespoons chopped fresh flat-leaf parsley leaves

Salt and freshly ground black pepper

---

1. Heat your grill to medium-high (page 3).

2. Place the wet corn on the grill, close the grill hood, and cook, turning once, for 15 to 20 minutes until steamed through and hot but still crisp (test by carefully piercing with a knife).

3. When the corn is cool enough to handle, strip off the husks and cut the kernels from the corncobs by standing them on end in a large bowl and cutting downward with a small knife. Place in a medium bowl and add the onion. Whisk the chipotle, lime juice, and oil together in a small bowl and pour over the corn mixture. Mix in the cilantro and parsley and season to taste with salt and pepper. Cover and refrigerate for at least 1 hour before serving. (*The relish can be made a few hours in advance, covered, and kept refrigerated.*)

FOR THE LOBSTER:

4 cedar planks (about 10 x 12 inches each), soaked in cold water for 1 hour

4 (8- to 10-ounce) lobster tails or 8 smaller tails, in the shell

Mild vegetable oil, such as canola

Salt and freshly ground black pepper

1. Heat your grill to medium-high (page 3).

2. Remove the planks from the water and place them on the grill to heat. Brush the lobster tails with oil and season with salt and pepper.

3. Arrange the tails meat side down on two of the planks (leave the planks on the grill). Using tongs, place the two remaining planks on top (the planks will be hot). Close the grill hood and cook until just cooked through, 12 to 15 minutes. Remove to a platter and top with corn relish. Serve immediately.

Serves 4; can be doubled for 6 to 8

Brick-Grilled Baby Squid
with Tamarind-Mint Dressing

When it's cooked just right, squid has an amazing texture—firm but tender. (If it's under-cooked or overcooked, it will be rubbery.) For perfect grilled squid, your most important cooking tool is a timer. All you have to do is stop cooking after 90 seconds!

I use a brick to press the squid down, so they cook quickly and evenly. With the lightly charred, smoky meat, I love a tart dressing with the sweetness of tamarind, but you could actually use any vinaigrette recipe in the book. Tamarind is commonly used in Indian cooking for a sweet-sour effect; you can order it at *www.kalustyan.com* or *www.ethnicgrocer.com*. These flavors are great alongside Tandoori Chicken skewers (page 98) or Tandoori-Marinated Rotisserie Cornish Hens (page 193).

FOR THE DRESSING:

¼ **cup orange juice, preferably fresh**

3 **tablespoons tamarind paste**
(available at Middle Eastern
and Indian markets; see headnote)

3 **tablespoons rice vinegar**

3 **tablespoons chopped fresh mint leaves**

1 **tablespoon Dijon mustard**

Salt and freshly ground black pepper

½ **cup peanut oil**

Combine the orange juice, tamarind, vinegar, mint, mustard, and salt and pepper to taste in a blender and blend until smooth. With the motor running, slowly add the oil and blend until emulsified. (Or combine all the ingredients in a jar with a tight-fitting lid and shake very well.) Taste for salt and pepper. *(The dressing can be made a day in advance, covered, and kept refrigerated. Bring to room temperature and whisk or shake well before serving.)*

FOR THE SQUID:

1½ pounds small squid bodies, cleaned
(buy them cleaned or have someone
at the fish counter clean them for you)
Olive oil
Salt and freshly ground black pepper
2 large bricks or other flat weights,
wrapped twice in aluminum foil
Chopped fresh mint leaves

1. Heat your grill to high (page 3).

2. Brush the squid with oil on both sides and season with salt and pepper. Place the squid close together on the grill and lay the bricks on the squid. Grill until lightly charred and cooked through, 4 to 5 minutes at the most. Do not turn them.

3. Remove the squid from the grill, slice into bite-size pieces if you wish, place on a platter, and drizzle with some of the dressing. Sprinkle with chopped mint. Serve hot or at room temperature.

Serves 4; can be doubled for 6 to 8 (no need to double the dressing)

Grilled Octopus–Sweet Onion Salad with Oregano Vinaigrette and Grilled Lemons

**BOBBY
FLAY'S
BOY
GETS
GRILL**

132

I wouldn't have pegged octopus as something I'd want to eat every day, but when I was in Greece that's exactly what I did. For me, lunch in the Greek islands always includes a plate of tender octopus dressed with plenty of lemon juice, olive oil, and fresh oregano— it's the best seafood salad there is. Adding "grilled" to the combination of bold flavors only makes it better, and the sweet onions add crunch.

Octopus must be boiled before grilling to tenderize it, and there's a tradition of boiling it with a few wine corks in the water, though no one seems to know why. (I've always done it that way, though, and the octopus comes out great.)

FOR THE OCTOPUS:

**2 pounds fresh or thawed frozen octopus
(not baby), cleaned (buy them cleaned
or have someone at the fish counter
clean them for you)**

2 tablespoons aged sherry vinegar

2 cloves garlic, smashed

10 wine corks (optional)

1 bay leaf

1 tablespoon black peppercorns

Bring a large pot of water to a rolling boil. Add the octopus, vinegar, garlic, corks, bay leaf, and peppercorns. Bring to a simmer and cook until tender, about 3 hours, adding more boiling water as needed to keep the octopus covered. Remove the octopus from the pot and drain on paper towels. *(The octopus can be boiled a day in advance, covered, and kept refrigerated. Bring to room temperature before proceeding.)*

FOR THE VINAIGRETTE:

2 cups fresh lemon juice

½ cup plus 1 tablespoon olive oil

½ shallot, coarsely chopped

1 clove garlic, chopped

1 teaspoon honey

Salt and freshly ground black pepper

2 tablespoons chopped fresh oregano leaves

1. Put the lemon juice in a medium saucepan (not cast-iron or aluminum) and simmer until reduced to ¼ cup.

2. Heat 1 tablespoon of the olive oil in a small skillet over medium heat and sauté the shallot and garlic until soft, about 5 minutes; do not brown.

3. Combine the lemon syrup, shallot mixture, and honey in a blender and blend until smooth. Add the remaining ½ cup olive oil a little at a time, blending until emulsified. Season to taste with salt and pepper. (*The vinaigrette can be made a few hours in advance, covered, and kept refrigerated. Bring to room temperature and whisk or shake well before serving.*) Just before serving, stir in the oregano by hand.

TO SERVE:

2 sweet onions, such as Vidalia or Walla Walla,
    sliced ½ inch thick

Olive oil

Salt and freshly ground black pepper

½ cup balsamic vinegar

4 lemons, halved crosswise

4 cups baby greens or mesclun

Chopped fresh oregano and flat-leaf parsley leaves

1. Heat your grill to high (page 3).

2. Brush the onion slices on both sides with oil and season with salt and pepper. Grill the onions, brushing with the vinegar every few minutes, until soft and caramelized, about 5 minutes on each side. Set aside.

3. Meanwhile brush the cut sides of the lemons with oil and place cut side down on the grill with the onions. Grill for 2 to 3 minutes, until lightly charred and heated through.

4. Brush the octopus with olive oil, season with salt and pepper, and grill until lightly charred and heated through, about 2 minutes on each side. Remove from the grill and cut into bite-size pieces.

5. Toss the greens in a large bowl with some of the vinaigrette and season to taste with salt and pepper. Spread the greens on a large platter and top with the octopus. Drizzle with more of the vinaigrette, top with the onion slices, and sprinkle with the fresh herbs. Serve immediately, garnishing each serving with grilled lemon.

Serves 4; can be doubled for 6 to 8

BOBBY
FLAY'S
BOY
GETS
GRILL

134

Grilled Whole Sardines
with Lemon, Olive Oil, and Black Pepper

I serve these delicious little grilled fish to my friends whenever I can get them, but I usually don't mention what they are. For some reason, the word "sardine" doesn't appeal to people. But these are so far away from the oily fish in a can; they're briny, rich, and crisp—a perfect backdrop for lemon, pepper, and the best olive oil you have.

¼ cup fresh lemon juice
¾ cup extra-virgin olive oil
1 teaspoon coarsely ground black pepper
12 fresh large white sardines, scaled and gutted,
    heads intact
Salt
3 tablespoons chopped fresh flat-leaf
    parsley leaves
2 lemons, quartered

1. Whisk together the lemon juice, ½ cup of the olive oil, and the pepper. Place the sardines in a medium dish, pour the dressing over them, turn to coat, and let marinate for 15 minutes.

2. Heat your grill to high (page 3).

3. Remove the sardines from the marinade and season them all over with salt. Grill until crisp, lightly charred, and just cooked through (page 5), 3 to 4 minutes on each side. Remove the sardines to a platter and sprinkle with the remaining ¼ cup olive oil and the parsley. Serve immediately with lemon wedges on the side.

Serves 4 as an appetizer; can be doubled for 6 to 8

Grilled Cod with Grilled Sweet Peppers and Parsley-Anchovy Relish

**BOBBY
FLAY'S
BOY
GETS
GRILL**

136

This powerful, irresistible relish of sweet peppers, strong anchovies, and fresh parsley is my reworking of Mediterranean peperonata, a classic salad/sauce/side dish that just explodes with flavor. It's great as a topping for mild white fish or all by itself on grilled bread. Grilling the peppers adds a smoky note that I love. Make the relish shortly before serving, or the anchovy flavor will overpower all the others.

White anchovies are called *boquerones* in Spain, from where they are imported. They are plumper, tastier, and less oily than regular anchovies. You can order oil-packed *boquerones* from *www.tienda.com* or substitute good-quality anchovy fillets.

FOR THE RELISH:

2 red bell peppers, roasted, peeled, seeded, and coarsely chopped (page 9)

2 yellow bell peppers, roasted, peeled, seeded, and coarsely chopped (page 9)

2 cloves garlic, minced

8 white anchovies (see headnote), coarsely chopped

½ cup extra-virgin olive oil

3 tablespoons red wine vinegar

¼ cup chopped fresh flat-leaf parsley leaves

1 tablespoon chopped fresh oregano leaves

Salt and freshly ground black pepper

Combine all the ingredients in a bowl and season to taste with salt and pepper. Set aside at room temperature for up to 30 minutes (see headnote).

FOR THE COD:

**4 (6- to 8-ounce) skinless cod fillets,
    1 to 1½ inches thick**
Olive oil
Salt and freshly ground black pepper

1. Heat your grill to high (page 3).

2. Brush the fish on both sides with oil and season with salt and pepper. Put the fish on the grill with the top side down (in other words, the side that will face up when you serve, so it should be the best-looking side). Grill the fish until lightly browned and firm on the bottom, 3 to 4 minutes. Turn the fillets over, reduce the heat to medium or move to a cooler part of the grill, and cook until just cooked through (page 5) but not falling apart, 2 to 3 minutes more.

3. Remove the fish to serving plates or a platter and top each piece with spoonfuls of the relish. Serve immediately.

Serves 4; can be doubled for 6 to 8

Grilled Cod with Tarragon, Yellow Tomato, and Black Olive Relish

BOBBY
FLAY'S
BOY
GETS
GRILL

138

Every few years I rediscover how much I like the flavor of tarragon, which is sort of a refreshing cross between celery and fennel. For me, one of the pleasures of cooking is forgetting about certain ingredients—just putting them on the bench for a while—so that when I take them out again they feel fresh and spark new ideas. That's how this tarragon-spiked recipe was born.

When I'm making a vegetable relish—a sort of combination salsa and salad—to put on top of a simple grilled fillet, I always think about color as well as flavor. The yellow tomato, magenta onion, black olives, and green tarragon here are especially striking.

FOR THE RELISH:

3 yellow tomatoes, cut into eighths
½ red onion, thinly sliced
½ cup Niçoise olives, pitted
½ cup extra-virgin olive oil
2 cloves garlic, finely chopped
2 tablespoons red wine vinegar
2 tablespoons finely chopped fresh
   tarragon leaves
Salt and freshly ground black pepper

Combine all the ingredients in a serving bowl and season to taste with salt and pepper. Set aside at room temperature for at least 30 minutes. *(The relish can be made a few hours in advance, covered, and kept refrigerated. Bring to room temperature before serving.)*

FOR THE COD:

4 (6- to 8-ounce) skinless fresh cod fillets,
   1 to 1½ inches thick
½ cup olive oil
¼ cup fresh tarragon leaves
Salt and freshly ground black pepper

1. Place the cod in a large dish or a sealable plastic bag. In a blender, purée the oil and tarragon together, pour over the cod, and turn to coat. Cover and refrigerate for 20 to 30 minutes.

2. Heat your grill to high (page 3).

3. Remove the fish from the marinade and season with salt and pepper. Put the fish on the grill with the top side down (in other words, the side that will face up when you serve, so it should be the best-looking side). Grill the fish until lightly browned and firm on the bottom, 3 to 4 minutes. Turn the fillets over, reduce the heat to medium or move to a cooler part of the grill, and cook until just cooked through (page 5) but not falling apart, 2 to 3 minutes more.

4. Remove the fish to serving plates or a platter and top each piece with spoonfuls of the relish. Serve immediately.

Serves 4; can be doubled for 6 to 8

Grilled Halibut with Mango, Serrano, and Scallion Relish

BOBBY
FLAY'S
BOY
GETS
GRILL

———

140

This is the kind of simple, lively dish that you can make for any occasion—or no occasion—all summer long. The spicy-sweet relish can be mixed well in advance; so while grilling the fish, just kick back and sip a tall glass of Fresh Lemonade with Tequila and Mint Sprigs (page 24).

Halibut is one of my favorite fish—I love that pearly white flesh and the way it stays moist on the grill—but you can substitute snapper, bass, or even flounder. Make sure to sprinkle plenty of salt on the fish just before grilling.

FOR THE RELISH:
2 ripe mangoes, peeled, pitted, and diced
6 scallions, thinly sliced
2 or 3 serrano chiles, seeded and minced
¼ cup fresh lime juice
2 tablespoons mild vegetable oil,
** such as canola**
¼ cup chopped fresh cilantro leaves
Salt and freshly ground black pepper

Combine all the ingredients in a bowl and season to taste with salt and pepper. Let sit at room temperature at least 30 minutes. (*The relish can be made a few hours in advance, covered, and kept refrigerated. Bring to room temperature before serving.*)

FOR THE HALIBUT:
4 (8-ounce) skinless halibut fillets,
** 1 to 1½ inches thick**
Mild vegetable oil, such as canola
Salt and freshly ground black pepper

1. Heat your grill to high (page 3).

2. Brush the fish on both sides with oil and season with salt and pepper. Put the fish on the grill with the top side down (in other words, the side that will face up when you serve, so it should be the best-looking side). Grill the fish until lightly browned and firm on the bottom, 3 to 4 minutes. Turn the fish over, reduce the heat to medium or move to a cooler part of the grill, and cook until just cooked through (page 5) but not falling apart, 2 to 3 minutes more.

3. Remove the fish to serving plates or a platter and top each piece with spoonfuls of the relish. Serve immediately.

Serves 4; can be doubled for 6 to 8

Grilled Halibut
with Grilled Peach-Mint-Balsamic Relish

BOBBY
FLAY'S
BOY
GETS
GRILL

142

Summer peaches aren't just for cobbler. I like to toss them on the grill and torch those natural sugars; high heat is essential for caramelizing the sugars without turning the peaches to mush. Dice them up with a fresh chile, add some bracing fresh mint and the sweet tang of balsamic vinegar, and the flavors come to life as the spice, sweet, and sour play off each other. A strong relish like this demands a mild fish like halibut; a fish with big flavors of its own would fight back.

FOR THE RELISH:

4 ripe peaches, halved and pitted

Mild vegetable oil, such as canola

½ red onion, thinly sliced

¼ cup coarsely chopped fresh mint leaves

1 jalapeño chile, seeded and minced

¼ cup extra-virgin olive oil

2 tablespoons balsamic vinegar

Salt and freshly ground black pepper

1. Heat your grill to high (page 3).

2. Brush the cut sides of the peaches with vegetable oil. Grill the peaches cut side down until browned, 2 to 3 minutes. Turn the peaches over and grill until soft, 2 to 3 minutes longer. Remove from the grill (leave the grill on if you'll be cooking the halibut right away).

3. When the peaches are cool enough to handle, coarsely chop, transfer to a bowl, and add the remaining relish ingredients. Season to taste with salt and pepper. *(The relish can be made a few hours in advance, covered, and kept refrigerated. Bring to room temperature before serving.)*

FOR THE HALIBUT:

4 (8-ounce) skinless halibut fillets,
1 to 1½ inches thick
Mild vegetable oil, such as canola
Salt and freshly ground black pepper

1. Heat your grill to high (page 3).

2. Brush the fish on both sides with oil and season with salt and pepper. Put the fish on the grill with the top side down (in other words, the side that will face up when you serve, so it should be the best-looking side). Grill the fish until lightly browned and firm on the bottom, 3 to 4 minutes. Turn the fish over, reduce the heat to medium or move to a cooler part of the grill, and cook until just cooked through (page 5) but not falling apart, 3 to 4 minutes more.

3. Remove the fish to serving plates or a platter and top each piece with spoonfuls of the relish. Serve immediately.

Serves 4; can be doubled for 6 to 8

Red Chile–Roasted Striped Bass
with Black Bean and Corn Succotash

BOBBY
FLAY'S
BOY
GETS
GRILL

144

This impressive dish is the perfect dinner for the end of summer, when corn is in season and fall is in the air. The succotash is hearty but not heavy, a delicious jumble of beans, corn, herbs, tomatoes, and (my favorite) bits of smoky bacon.

Make sure to marinate the fish at the last minute, because the strong marinade could start to "cook" the fish in the citrus juice.

FOR THE SUCCOTASH:
1 cup fresh or thawed frozen lima beans
8 slices bacon, diced
4 tablespoons unsalted butter
2 scallions, thinly sliced
1 cup canned black beans, rinsed and drained
1 cup clam juice
1 cup vegetable stock
2 teaspoons chipotle purée (page 12)
Kernels from 2 ears of corn,
    or 1½ cups thawed frozen corn kernels
8 ounces cherry tomatoes, halved,
    or diced fresh tomatoes
2 tablespoons chopped fresh cilantro leaves
Salt and freshly ground black pepper

1. Cook the lima beans in boiling salted water until tender all the way through, about 10 minutes. Drain well.

2. Meanwhile heat a deep skillet over medium heat. Add the bacon and cook slowly until well browned and the fat is rendered, about 10 minutes. Use a slotted spoon to remove the bacon to a plate lined with paper towels.

3. Pour off all but 1 tablespoon of the bacon fat from the skillet and place the pan back on the heat. Add 2 tablespoons of the butter (keep the remaining 2 tablespoons refrigerated) and the scallions; cook, stirring, until the scallions soften. Add the lima beans, black beans, clam juice, stock, and chipotle purée. Bring to a simmer and cook for 10 minutes

4. Remove the bean mixture from the heat and stir in the cooked bacon, corn, tomatoes, cold butter, and cilantro and season with salt and pepper to taste. The succotash will be slightly soupy. Serve warm or hot. *(The succotash can be made a day in advance, covered, and kept refrigerated. Reheat before serving.)*

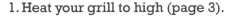

FOR THE BASS:

2 ancho chiles, soaked in hot water to cover for 1 hour

1 cup fresh orange juice

½ cup fresh lime juice

Salt

4 (8-ounce) striped bass fillets, preferably wild, about 1 inch thick

Freshly ground black pepper

Fresh flat-leaf parsley leaves

1. Heat your grill to high (page 3).

2. Remove the ancho chiles from their soaking liquid and discard the stems and seeds, reserving the liquid. Coarsely chop the chiles and place in a blender with the orange juice, lime juice, and 3 tablespoons of the soaking liquid. Blend, adding more liquid if needed to make a smooth purée, and season to taste with salt. Place the fish in a large dish and pour the marinade over it. Turn the fillets to coat, cover, and refrigerate for 10 minutes, no longer.

3. Remove the fish from the marinade and season with salt and pepper. Put the fish on the grill with the top side down (in other words, the side that will face up when you serve, so it should be the best-looking side). Grill the fish until lightly browned and firm on the bottom, 3 to 4 minutes. Turn the fish over, reduce the heat to medium or move to a cooler part of the grill, and cook until just cooked through (page 5) but not falling apart, 3 to 4 minutes more.

4. Divide the hot succotash in shallow serving bowls. Place the fish on top, sprinkle with parsley, and serve immediately.

Serves 4; can be doubled for 6 to 8

Grilled Salmon
with Crunchy Sweet Mustard Vinaigrette

BOBBY
FLAY'S
BOY
GETS
GRILL

146

I don't know if it's because of all the hot dogs I ate on the sidewalks of New York as a kid, but I never seem to get tired of mustard. I use it as a background flavor in a lot of my sauces, but in this one mustard is front and center. The sharpness of mustard, which is simply a purée of vinegar, mustard seeds, and salt, works well with a rich, sweet fish like salmon. Use a whole-grain mustard, such as Pommery de Meaux from France, so that your sauce has a nice crunch from the whole seeds. Because mustard seeds are often used in Indian cooking, this dish is particularly good with Coconut-Cashew Basmati Rice Salad (page 76).

FOR THE VINAIGRETTE:
3 tablespoons white wine vinegar
2 tablespoons coarse-
    or whole-grain Dijon mustard
1 small shallot, finely chopped
2 tablespoons honey
½ cup olive oil
Salt and freshly ground black pepper

Whisk the vinegar, mustard, and shallot together in a medium bowl. Gradually whisk in the honey, then the oil, until the dressing is emulsified. Season to taste with salt and pepper. *(The vinaigrette can be made a few hours in advance, covered, and kept refrigerated. Bring to room temperature and whisk or shake well before serving.)*

FOR THE SALMON:
4 (6- to 8-ounce) salmon fillets,
    1 to 1½ inches thick, with the skin
Olive oil
Salt and freshly ground black pepper

1. Heat your grill to high (page 3).

2. Brush the fish on both sides with oil and season with salt and pepper. Grill the salmon skin side down until the skin is lightly charred and crisp, 4 to 5 minutes. Turn the fillets over, reduce the heat to medium or move to a cooler part of the grill, and cook until just cooked through (page 5) but not falling apart, 2 to 3 minutes more.

3. Remove the fish to serving plates or a platter and spoon a few tablespoons of vinaigrette over each fillet. Serve immediately.

Serves 4; can be doubled for 6 to 8

Grilled Salmon
with Tomato-Caper Vinaigrette

BOBBY
FLAY'S
BOY
GETS
GRILL

148

This tangy, fresh-tasting dish is easily made with pantry staples as long as you have fresh salmon, summer herbs, and a couple of ripe beefsteak tomatoes. Serve it with a chilled, dry rosé from France or Spain to complement the bright Mediterranean flavors.

Although many chefs like to serve salmon with a raw center, I prefer it just cooked through.

FOR THE VINAIGRETTE:

3 ripe beefsteak tomatoes, cored, seeded, and diced

¼ red onion, finely chopped

2 tablespoons capers, drained

¼ cup aged sherry vinegar

½ cup extra-virgin olive oil

2 teaspoons finely chopped fresh thyme leaves

2 tablespoons chopped fresh basil leaves

Salt and freshly ground black pepper

Combine all the ingredients in a medium bowl and season with salt and pepper to taste. Let sit at room temperature for at least 30 minutes. (*The vinaigrette can be made up to 2 hours in advance and kept refrigerated. Bring to room temperature and mix well before serving.*)

FOR THE SALMON:

4 (8-ounce) salmon fillets, 1 to 1½ inches thick, with the skin

Canola oil

Salt and freshly ground black pepper

1. Heat your grill to medium-high (page 3).

2. Brush the fish on both sides with oil and season with salt and pepper. Grill the salmon skin side down until the skin is lightly charred and crisp, 3 to 4 minutes. Turn the fillets

over, reduce the heat to medium or move to a cooler part of the grill, and cook until just cooked through (page 5) but not falling apart, 3 to 4 minutes more.

3. Remove the fish to serving plates or a platter and spoon a few tablespoons of vinaigrette over each fillet. Serve immediately.

Serves 4; can be doubled for 6 to 8

Grilled Tuna with Red Chile, Allspice, and Orange Glaze

Anchos are the dried chiles I use most for they have the best balance of fruity, spicy, and earthy flavors. Ancho powder gives this glaze its appealing brick-red color and warm—not fiery—flavor. I definitely find that tuna needs intense flavors, like orange and allspice, to lighten it up and show off that meaty texture.

Serve this dish with a hearty salad like Grilled Asparagus and Quinoa Salad with Goat Cheese and Spicy Black Olive Vinaigrette (page 82).

FOR THE GLAZE:

3 cups orange juice

3 tablespoons rice vinegar

2 teaspoons ground allspice

1 tablespoon ancho chile powder

½ cup mild vegetable oil, such as canola

Salt and freshly ground black pepper

1. Place the orange juice in a medium saucepan (not aluminum or cast-iron) and boil until reduced to ½ cup.

2. Transfer the orange syrup to a blender, add the vinegar, allspice, and ancho powder, and blend until combined. With the motor running, slowly add the oil and process until emulsified. Season to taste with salt and pepper. (*The glaze can be made a few days in advance, covered, and kept refrigerated. Bring to room temperature before serving.*)

FOR THE TUNA:

**4 (8-ounce) tuna fillets or steaks,
 1 to 1½ inches thick**

Mild vegetable oil, such as canola

Salt and freshly ground black pepper

1. Heat your grill to high (page 3).

2. Set aside a few tablespoons of glaze for brushing the cooked fish. Brush the fish on both sides with oil and season with salt and pepper. Put the fish on the grill with the top side down (in other words, the side that will face up when you serve, so it should be the best-looking side). Grill the fish until crusty and browned on the bottom, about 2 minutes. Turn the fish over and grill, brushing the top frequently with the glaze, until medium-rare (page 5), 2 to 3 minutes longer.

3. Remove the fish from the grill and brush on both sides with the reserved glaze. Serve immediately.

Serves 4; can be doubled for 6 to 8 (no need to double the glaze)

FISH AND SHELLFISH

Grilled Tuna
with Avocado-Tomatillo Sauce

BOBBY
FLAY'S
BOY
GETS
GRILL

152

In New York all my favorite Latin cafés—whether they're making Cuban sandwiches, Venezuelan empanadas, or Mexican tacos—keep a special, house-made hot sauce tucked behind the counter. (Bottled hot sauce is on the table, but you have to ask for the good stuff.) It's delicious, sometimes fiery hot, but always green and aromatic with garlic, fresh herbs, lime juice, and minced onion. I liked them so much that I finally had to invent my own.

Tart tomatillos, hot jalapeño, fresh lime, and sweet honey, all bound together with the creaminess of avocado, make this one of my favorite sauces. Try it on any rich fish, like swordfish, salmon, mackerel, or bluefish. To use it as a smooth dipping sauce, as in the picture on page 15 of the photograph insert, add the avocado, onion, and cilantro to the blender with the other ingredients and purée until smooth.

FOR THE SAUCE:

8 tomatillos, husked and rinsed

2 jalapeño chiles

½ cup mild vegetable oil, such as canola,
   plus extra for brushing

Salt and freshly ground black pepper

¼ cup fresh lime juice

2 tablespoons honey

4 ripe Hass avocados, halved, pitted, peeled,
   and cut into ½-inch dice

1 small red onion, finely diced

¼ cup chopped fresh cilantro leaves

---

1. Heat your grill to high (page 3).

2. Brush the tomatillos and chiles with oil and season all over with salt and pepper. Grill the tomatillos and chiles, turning, until blackened on all sides. Remove from the grill (leave the grill on if you'll be cooking the fish right away) and coarsely chop the tomatillos. Stem, seed, and chop the chiles.

3. Combine the tomatillos, chiles, lime juice, and honey in a blender and blend until smooth. With the motor running, gradually pour in the ½ cup oil and blend until emulsified. Transfer to a bowl and fold in the avocados, onion, and cilantro. Season to taste with salt and pepper. *(The sauce can be made 2 hours in advance, covered, and kept refrigerated. Bring to room temperature before serving.)*

FOR THE TUNA:

4 (8-ounce) tuna fillets or steaks,
1 to 1½ inches thick
Mild vegetable oil, such as canola
Salt and freshly ground black pepper

1. Heat your grill to high (page 3).

2. Brush the fish on both sides with oil and season with salt and pepper. Put the fish on the grill with the top side down (in other words, the side that will face up when you serve, so it should be the best-looking side). Grill the fish until crusty and browned on the bottom, about 3 minutes. Turn the fish over and grill until medium-rare (page 5), 2 to 3 minutes longer.

3. Remove the fish from the grill and spoon the sauce over each piece. Serve immediately.

Serves 4; can be doubled for 6 to 8

Grilled Tuna with Grilled Mushrooms in Sherry Vinaigrette

BOBBY
FLAY'S
BOY
GETS
GRILL

154

Though it's not an obvious combination, I love the earthiness of mushrooms with a rich fish like tuna or with meaty sea scallops. These shiitakes are grilled, sliced, and then marinated in an herbal, mustardy vinaigrette. They add major flavor to a fish that can be too mild on its own; all you have to do is add a mound of Grilled Vegetable–Saffron Rice Salad (page 78; go light on the dressing), sit back, and collect the compliments. The flavors are particularly well suited to a fall dinner.

FOR THE SAUCE:

6 shiitake mushrooms, stems removed

½ cup olive oil, plus extra for brushing

Salt and freshly ground black pepper

1 small shallot, chopped

1 tablespoon Dijon mustard

¼ cup aged sherry vinegar

2 tablespoons chopped fresh flat-leaf parsley leaves

1 tablespoon finely chopped fresh thyme leaves

1. Heat your grill to high (page 3).

2. Brush the mushroom caps on both sides with oil and season with salt and pepper. Grill for 3 to 4 minutes on each side, until just cooked through. Remove from the grill. When the mushrooms are cool enough to handle, thinly slice them.

3. Whisk together the shallot, mustard, and vinegar in a large bowl. Gradually whisk in the ½ cup olive oil until emulsified and season to taste with salt and pepper. Fold in the mushrooms, parsley, and thyme. Set aside at room temperature for at least 20 minutes. (The sauce can be made up to 2 hours in advance, covered, and set aside at room temperature.)

FOR THE TUNA:

**4 (8-ounce) tuna fillets or steaks,
1 to 1½ inches thick**

Olive oil

Salt and freshly ground black pepper

Fresh flat-leaf parsley leaves

1. Heat your grill to high (page 3).

2. Brush the fish on both sides with oil and season with salt and pepper. Put the fish on the grill with the top side down (in other words, the side that will face up when you serve, so it should be the best-looking side). Grill the fish until crusty and browned on the bottom, about 2 minutes. Turn the fish over and grill until medium-rare (page 5), 2 to 3 minutes longer.

3. Remove the fish to serving plates or a platter. Spoon the mushroom sauce over each piece, sprinkle with parsley leaves, and serve immediately.

Serves 4; can be doubled for 6 to 8

Jerk-Rubbed Swordfish
with Habanero-Mint Glaze

BOBBY
FLAY'S
BOY
GETS
GRILL

156

The best jerk I ever had wasn't in Jamaica: it was in Brooklyn, at the annual West Indian Day Parade, an unbelievable blast of music, costume, colors, and food. People with roots in the Caribbean come from all corners of the city, and I believe it's for the food more than anything. The grills are lit early in the morning to begin laying down the bed of hot coals you need to make real Jamaican jerk.

Bold jerk spices work really well with the meatiness of swordfish. This isn't one of those delicate fish dishes; it's more like a smoky, spicy barbecue experience!

FOR THE RUB:

2 tablespoons ground coriander

2 tablespoons ground ginger

2 tablespoons light brown sugar

1 tablespoon onion powder

1 tablespoon garlic powder

1 tablespoon salt

2 teaspoons habanero chile powder
    or cayenne

2 teaspoons coarsely ground black pepper

2 teaspoons dried thyme

1 teaspoon ground cinnamon

1 teaspoon ground allspice

1 teaspoon ground cloves

Combine all the ingredients in a bowl or a jar with a tight-fitting lid and mix well. *(The rub keeps well for months stored at room temperature in a jar with a tight-fitting lid.)*

FOR THE GLAZE:

2 cups red wine vinegar

2 cups white wine vinegar

3 cups sugar

2 habanero or serrano chiles,
    seeded and coarsely chopped
½ cup fresh mint leaves, coarsely chopped
Salt

1. Combine the vinegars and sugar in a medium saucepan (not aluminum or cast-iron) and boil over medium-high heat, stirring often. Cook until thickened and reduced by three-quarters to about 1 cup liquid. Let cool.

2. Transfer the vinegar syrup to a blender, add the habaneros and mint, and blend until smooth. Season to taste with salt and let cool to room temperature. (*The glaze can be made and kept refrigerated up to 2 days in advance. Bring to room temperature and whisk or shake well before serving.*)

FOR THE SWORDFISH:
4 (8-ounce) swordfish fillets or steaks,
    1 to 1½ inches thick
Mild vegetable oil, such as canola

1. Heat your grill to high (page 3). Set aside a few tablespoons of glaze for brushing the cooked fish.

2. Brush the fish on one side with oil. Rub the other side of each piece of fish with 1 tablespoon of the rub and drizzle with oil.

3. Put the fish rub side down on the grill and cook until seared and crusty, 2 to 3 minutes. Turn the fish over, reduce the heat to medium or move to a cooler part of the grill, and brush with the glaze. Grill, brushing often with the glaze, until just cooked all the way through (page 5), 3 to 4 minutes more.

4. Remove the fish to a platter, brush with the reserved glaze, and serve immediately.

Serves 4; can be doubled for 6 to 8 (no need to double the rub or glaze)

Grilled Swordfish with Coconut, Key Lime, and Green Chile Sauce

With its irresistible coconut-rich, lime-tart sauce, this plate is where the Caribbean meets Thailand. Coconut, lime, chiles, ginger, and cilantro are used all the time in both cuisines. I love coconut milk; it's so rich and flavorful that it's almost a sauce in itself. Try this sauce on grilled shrimp or scallops, too.

FOR THE SAUCE:

1 (14-ounce) can unsweetened coconut milk

2 tablespoons canned cream of coconut

2 teaspoons grated lime zest

¼ cup fresh or bottled lime juice,
      preferably key lime

4 serrano chiles, seeded and chopped

1 (1-inch) piece fresh ginger, peeled
      and chopped

½ cup mild vegetable oil, such as canola

¼ cup shredded unsweetened dried coconut

2 tablespoons chopped fresh cilantro leaves

Salt and freshly ground black pepper

Combine the coconut milk, cream of coconut, lime zest, lime juice, chiles, and ginger in a blender and blend until smooth. With the motor running, slowly pour in the oil and blend until emulsified. Pour the mixture into a bowl and stir in the coconut and cilantro. Season to taste with salt and pepper. *(The sauce can be made a few hours in advance, covered, and kept refrigerated. Bring to room temperature before serving.)*

FOR THE SWORDFISH:

4 (8-ounce) swordfish steaks,
      1 to 1½ inches thick

Mild vegetable oil, such as canola

Salt and freshly ground black pepper
Shredded unsweetened dried coconut,
    lightly toasted (page 10)
Chopped fresh cilantro leaves

1. Heat your grill to high (page 3).

2. Brush the fish on both sides with oil and season with salt and pepper. Grill the fish until crusty and browned on the bottom, 3 to 4 minutes. Turn the fish over, reduce the heat to medium or move to a cooler part of the grill, and grill until just cooked all the way through (page 5), 3 to 4 minutes more.

3. Remove the fish to serving plates or a platter. Drizzle with the coconut sauce, garnish with coconut and cilantro, and serve immediately.

Serves 4; can be doubled for 6 to 8 (no need to double the sauce)

**FISH
AND
SHELLFISH**

Grilled Whole Fish with Tarragon, Orange, and Parsley

BOBBY
FLAY'S
BOY
GETS
GRILL

160

A whole fish is one of the most impressive things to serve—and one of the easiest things to grill. You can use one of those specially designed fish holders to turn the fish, but I find that a large spatula and a little practice works even better. A 2-pound fish is a very manageable size that cooks through quickly, stays moist, and develops a crisp skin that's full of flavor. For the crispiest skin, cut three slashes in the skin on both sides of the fish when you turn it over. When you drizzle the vinaigrette on the hot fish, the perfume will almost knock you out—in a good way!

Removing the fish from the bones is easy: Just make one long cut all the way down the backbone of the fish. Then use a fork to gently slide the meat along the bones, pushing toward the belly of the fish. Once the meat is away from the bones, you can easily lift it up and serve. To get at the meat on the other side, gently pull up the skeleton of the fish with your fingers until it comes away, or turn the whole fish over with a wide spatula and repeat the above procedure.

FOR THE VINAIGRETTE:
¼ cup aged sherry vinegar
1 small shallot, chopped
2 teaspoons Dijon mustard
3 tablespoons chopped tarragon leaves
Salt and freshly ground black pepper
½ cup olive oil

Whisk the vinegar, shallot, mustard, tarragon, and salt and pepper to taste in a medium bowl. Gradually whisk in the oil until emulsified. *(The vinaigrette can be made a few hours in advance, covered, and kept refrigerated. Bring to room temperature and whisk or shake well before serving.)*

FOR THE FISH:
2 (2-pound) whole red snappers, striped bass,
   or black sea bass, scaled and gutted

Olive oil

Salt and freshly ground black pepper

1 large orange, thinly sliced

1 bunch fresh tarragon

1 bunch fresh flat-leaf parsley

1. Make sure the grate of your grill is well oiled and heat to high (page 3).

2. Brush the fish on both sides with olive oil and season with salt and pepper. Stuff the fish with orange slices, tarragon, and parsley.

3. Grill the fish for 4 to 5 minutes. Carefully turn the fish over (use a large spatula), reduce the heat to medium or move to a cooler part of the grill, close the grill hood, and grill for 6 to 7 minutes more, until just cooked through (page 5).

4. Remove the fish to a platter and drizzle with the vinaigrette. Serve immediately.

Serves 4; can be doubled for 6 to 8 (no need to double the dressing)

Grilled Whole Fish with Oregano Salt and Black Olive–Feta Relish

With the herbal punch of fresh oregano and the freshness of lemon, this takes me right back to an oceanfront taverna in the Greek islands—or at least to Queens, where there are wonderful Greek seafood restaurants that have imported the old-country skill of grilling whole fish. As you're waiting to be seated, you get to pick out the fattest, freshest fish for your own dinner from the refrigerated cases up front.

The tangy, salty feta-and-olive topping I created for this dish has become one of my favorites. It's too creamy to be a salsa, too chunky to be a sauce, but whatever you call it, it perfectly complements the big, white flakes of grilled snapper.

FOR THE RELISH:

1 cup crumbled feta

½ cup Kalamata olives, pitted and chopped

1 tablespoon chopped fresh oregano leaves

**3 tablespoons extra-virgin olive oil,
plus extra if needed**

Freshly ground black pepper

Combine the feta, olives, and oregano in a bowl, add the olive oil, and carefully fold the ingredients together. If needed add a little more olive oil to bind the mixture together. Season to taste with pepper and set aside. *(The relish can be made a few hours in advance, covered, and kept refrigerated. Bring to room temperature before serving.)*

FOR THE FISH:

**4 (1-pound) whole red snappers, striped bass,
or sea bass, or 2 (2-pound) fish, scaled
and gutted**

Olive oil

**3 tablespoons coarse sea salt,
or 2 tablespoons kosher salt**

1 tablespoon grated lemon zest

3 tablespoons chopped fresh oregano leaves

2 lemons, sliced ¼ inch thick

1. Make sure the grate of your grill is well oiled and heat to high (page 3).

2. Brush the fish all over with olive oil. In a small bowl, mix together the salt, lemon zest, and oregano. Season the fish, including the cavities, with the salt mixture. Place a few slices of lemon in each cavity.

3. Place the fish on the grill and cook until lightly charred, 3 to 4 minutes for smaller fish or about 5 minutes for larger ones. Carefully turn the fish over (use a large spatula), reduce the heat to medium or move to a cooler part of the grill, close the grill hood, and grill for 4 to 5 minutes more for smaller fish and 6 to 7 minutes for larger ones, until just cooked through (page 5).

4. Remove the fish to a platter or serving plates and use a small knife to cut all the way down the backbone of the fish (this will make it easier for guests to slide the meat off the bones). Spoon the feta relish on top and serve immediately.

Serves 4; can be doubled for 6 to 8

CHICKEN, DUCK, AND OTHER BIRDS

Caribbean-Spiced Chicken with Mango Yogurt Sauce

BOBBY
FLAY'S
BOY
GETS
GRILL

166

Somewhere in the Caribbean, someone is kicking back with a plate of chicken that tastes a lot like this. It has some of the flavors and heat of Jamaican jerk, but it's as easy as plain grilled chicken. The garlic and spices permeate the meat once you paint on a sweet-tart spice paste that also tenderizes (thanks to the vinegar and lime juice).

This is a dish you can marinate—and even grill—well in advance and serve later at room temperature. The sweet yogurt, with its chunks of juicy mango, cools off the spices. I'd serve this dish with tequila-spiked fresh lemonade (page 24) poured over ice.

FOR THE CHICKEN:

10 scallions, white and pale green
    parts only, coarsely chopped
4 cloves garlic, chopped
1 (2-inch) piece fresh ginger, peeled
    and chopped
1 habanero or serrano chile, seeded
    and chopped
½ cup white wine vinegar
1 tablespoon fresh lime juice
1 tablespoon soy sauce
2 tablespoons light brown sugar
3 tablespoons chopped fresh
    cilantro leaves
2 tablespoons chopped fresh
    thyme leaves
½ teaspoon ground allspice
Salt and freshly ground black pepper
1 (4-pound) chicken, cut into
    8 serving pieces

Combine the scallions, garlic, ginger, chile, vinegar, lime juice, soy sauce, brown sugar, cilantro, thyme, and allspice in a blender and blend until smooth. Season to taste with salt and pepper. Place the chicken in a large dish, pour the marinade over it, and turn to coat the chicken. Cover and refrigerate for at least 8 hours and up to 24 hours. Remove from the refrigerator 30 minutes before cooking.

CHICKEN,
DUCK,
AND
OTHER
BIRDS

167

FOR THE YOGURT SAUCE:
1 ripe mango, peeled and pitted
2 cups thick yogurt (page 12)
3 scallions, thinly sliced
Salt and freshly ground black pepper

Purée the mango flesh in a food processor or blender (you might need to add a little water to make a smooth purée). Transfer to a bowl, mix in the remaining ingredients, and season to taste with salt and pepper. (*The sauce can be made up to 2 hours in advance, covered, and kept refrigerated. Mix well before serving.*)

TO SERVE:
Fresh cilantro leaves and quartered limes

1. Heat your grill to medium (page 3). Remove the chicken from the marinade and season all over with salt and pepper.

2. Put the chicken skin side down on the grate and grill until golden brown and lightly charred, 8 to 10 minutes. Turn the chicken over, reduce the heat to medium or move to a cooler part of the grill, close the grill hood, and cook until cooked through, 4 to 5 minutes more for wings, 8 to 10 minutes more for breasts, 10 to 12 minutes more for legs and thighs.

3. Remove the chicken to a platter, garnish with cilantro and limes, and serve immediately. Pass the yogurt sauce separately.

Serves 4; can be doubled for 6 to 8 (no need to double the marinade or the sauce)

Jerk-Rubbed Chicken Thighs
with Homemade Habanero Hot Sauce

BOBBY
FLAY'S
BOY
GETS
GRILL

168

I know there are lots of you hot sauce fans out there, but did you know that you can make your own? It's incredibly easy and has a superb fresh flavor that you can't get from a bottle. With homemade hot sauce, you can really taste the fruit of the chiles as well as the fire. The habaneros have a special taste that I love; the chile is characteristic of Caribbean hot sauces, making this a great choice for some spicy-sweet jerk chicken.

FOR THE SAUCE:

2 tablespoons mild vegetable oil,
    such as canola
1 small onion, finely chopped
2 cloves garlic, finely chopped
2 ripe mangoes, peeled, pitted,
    and coarsely chopped
2 habanero or serrano chiles, seeded
    and chopped
1 tablespoon honey, or more to taste
1 cup white wine vinegar, or more
    to taste
Salt

1. Heat the oil in a medium saucepan over medium-high heat. Add the onion and garlic and cook, stirring, until soft, about 8 minutes; do not brown. Add the mangoes and habaneros and cook for 10 minutes, stirring often. Add the honey and vinegar and simmer until slightly thickened, 15 to 20 minutes.

2. Transfer the mango mixture to a blender and blend until smooth. Strain into a bowl. If the mixture is too thick to pour, add a few tablespoons of warm water. Season to taste with salt, vinegar, and honey. (*The sauce can be made up to a day in advance, covered, and kept refrigerated. Bring to room temperature and mix well before serving.*)

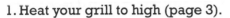

FOR THE CHICKEN:

**8 to 10 skin-on chicken thighs,
   preferably boneless**

Salt

½ cup jerk rub (page 156)

Mild vegetable oil, such as canola

Mango slices

Fresh cilantro leaves

**CHICKEN,
DUCK,
AND
OTHER
BIRDS**

169

1. Heat your grill to high (page 3).

2. Season the chicken all over with salt. Rub the skin of the chicken with plenty of spice rub. Drizzle with oil and place the thighs skin side down on the grate. Grill until the skin is golden brown and crusty, 4 to 5 minutes. Turn the chicken over, reduce the heat to medium or move to a cooler part of the grill, close the grill hood, and cook until just cooked through (page 5), about 4 minutes more (bone-in thighs will take longer).

3. Remove the chicken to a platter, garnish with mango and cilantro, and serve immediately. Pass the sauce separately.

Serves 4; can be doubled for 6 to 8

Soy-Ginger Chicken Rolled in Crisp Lettuce with Peanut Dipping Sauce

I always like food that's rolled, wrapped, or folded, like tacos, Peking duck, dumplings, empanadas, gyros—the list takes you around the world, not to mention around New York! They're perfect for eating outdoors. (Actually, I've never been to China or Caracas, but I feel I've eaten there thanks to New York's international restaurants and markets.)

In Vietnam (which I learned about by eating in Chinatown), hot food such as grilled beef or fried spring rolls is often rolled up in cool, crisp lettuce leaves with large sprigs of mint and cilantro. The contrast between the hot, spicy, charred food and the cooling, fresh greens is fantastic.

To set up, place all the herbs and greens on a big platter in the middle of the table and pour the sauce into small individual bowls for dipping. If you want a lighter sauce, try a traditional Vietnamese one of rice vinegar, Asian fish sauce, chile flakes, lime juice, and sugar—mixed to taste.

FOR THE GLAZE:
2 tablespoons peanut oil
1 (2-inch) piece fresh ginger, peeled
    and finely chopped
8 cloves garlic, finely chopped
¼ cup soy sauce
¾ cup honey
Freshly ground black pepper

Heat the oil in a saucepan over medium-high heat. Add the ginger and garlic and cook, stirring, until soft, about 5 minutes; do not brown. Stir in the soy sauce and honey and simmer for just a minute until the honey is melted. Turn off the heat, let cool slightly, and season to taste with pepper. (*The glaze can be made a few days in advance, covered, and kept refrigerated. Bring to room temperature before proceeding.*)

FOR THE SAUCE:

1 cup smooth natural peanut butter

½ cup water

3 tablespoons soy sauce

2 tablespoons rice vinegar

1 tablespoon toasted sesame oil

2 cloves garlic, chopped

1 (1-inch) piece fresh ginger, peeled
   and chopped

2 tablespoons chopped roasted peanuts

CHICKEN,
DUCK,
AND
OTHER
BIRDS

171

Combine the peanut butter, water, soy sauce, vinegar, sesame oil, garlic, and ginger in a food processor or blender and process until smooth. (Or whisk together in a bowl.) *(The sauce can be made a few hours in advance, covered, and kept refrigerated. Bring to room temperature before serving.)* Serve the sauce in individual bowls for dipping, garnished with peanuts.

FOR THE CHICKEN:

8 skinless, boneless chicken thighs,
   cut in half

32 wooden skewers, soaked in water
   for 30 minutes

Mild vegetable oil, such as canola

Salt and freshly ground black pepper

16 (6-inch) flour tortillas, stacked
   and wrapped in foil

Fresh cilantro leaves

Fresh mint leaves

Bibb or Boston lettuce leaves

1. Heat your grill to high (page 3).

2. To help the chicken stay flat while cooking, place two skewers next to each other, about ½ inch apart, and thread one piece of chicken lengthwise onto them. Repeat

with the remaining chicken and skewers. Brush the chicken with oil and season with salt and pepper.

3. Grill the chicken until browned and crusty, about 4 minutes. Turn the skewers over, and reduce the heat to medium or move to a cooler part of the grill. Cook, brushing often with the glaze, until just cooked through (page 5), about 4 minutes more.

4. While the chicken is cooking, place the foil package of tortillas on the grill to heat through, about 5 minutes.

5. Remove the chicken to a platter. Serve on or off the skewers. To eat, roll two pieces of chicken with cilantro, mint, and lettuce in a tortilla and dip the rolls in the sauce.

Serves 4; can be doubled for 6 to 8 (no need to double the sauce)

CHICKEN,
DUCK,
AND
OTHER
BIRDS

Grilled Chicken with Toasted Chiles, Coconut Milk, Lime, and Crushed Peanuts

BOBBY
FLAY'S
BOY
GETS
GRILL

174

One of my favorite New York shops is Kitchen Market, a little place in Chelsea where they know everything about chiles. Going to places where the owners really know and care about their stuff makes shopping for food a pleasure instead of a chore—and fortunately, New York is full of them!

This dish is a little Southwestern, a little Asian, a little Caribbean, and all flavor. The sauce, with its spicy, sweet, creamy, and citrus flavors, transforms a quick grilled chicken breast recipe into something intriguing and delicious.

FOR THE SAUCE:

3 dried New Mexico chiles

2 tablespoons mild vegetable oil, such as canola

1 small red onion, coarsely chopped

3 cloves garlic, coarsely chopped

2 teaspoons turmeric

1 (14-ounce) can unsweetened coconut milk

¼ cup canned cream of coconut

Juice of 1 lime, or more to taste

1 tablespoon honey

Salt and freshly ground black pepper

1. Heat your grill to high (page 3) or heat a heavy skillet on the stove.

2. Place the chiles on the grill and toast on each side for 20 seconds. Remove from the grill, discard the chile stems and seeds, and coarsely chop the chiles. Leave the grill on if you'll be cooking the chicken right away.

3. Heat the oil in a saucepan over medium-high heat. Add the onion and garlic and cook, stirring, until soft, about 7 minutes; do not brown. Add the turmeric and cook for 1 minute. Add the coconut milk, cream of coconut, and chiles and cook for 10 minutes.

4. Transfer the mixture to a blender and blend until smooth, or use a handheld blender in the pot. Add the lime juice and honey and blend again. Strain the mixture into a bowl and season to taste with lime juice, salt, and pepper. *(The sauce can be made a day in advance, covered, and kept refrigerated. Rewarm before serving.)*

**CHICKEN,
DUCK,
AND
OTHER
BIRDS**

175

FOR THE CHICKEN:

¾ **cup roasted peanuts, coarsely chopped**

3 tablespoons chopped fresh cilantro leaves

8 skinless, boneless chicken breast halves

Olive oil

Salt and freshly ground black pepper

1. Heat your grill to high (page 3).

2. Combine the peanuts and cilantro in a bowl and toss together. Brush the chicken on both sides with oil and season with salt and pepper.

3. Grill the chicken until browned and firm, about 3 minutes. Turn the breasts over, reduce the heat to medium or move to a cooler part of the grill, and cook until just cooked through (page 5), about 3 minutes more.

4. Remove the chicken to a platter or serving plates and drizzle with the sauce. Sprinkle the peanut-cilantro mixture over the chicken and serve immediately.

Serves 4; can be doubled for 6 to 8 (no need to double the sauce)

Spanish-Spiced Chicken
with Tangy Pomegranate-Mustard Glaze

BOBBY
FLAY'S
BOY
GETS
GRILL

176

Pomegranate molasses is the American name for an ancient Mediterranean ingredient, concentrated pomegranate juice. It has a complex, tart, bittersweet flavor that echoes some of my other favorite ingredients: balsamic vinegar, chipotle chiles in adobo, brown sugar, and, of course, molasses. I first tasted it as a mysterious, sweet-and-sour ingredient in my favorite salads from Kalustyan's, a fabulous Middle Eastern market in New York's Curry Hill neighborhood.

Bright-red, super-sweet grenadine is also made from pomegranate juice, but pomegranate molasses is different—dark, puckery, and almost smoky. Its sweetness makes it a natural glaze for crisp chicken skin, and it stands up well to the powerful spices in this potent rub. You can order pomegranate molasses from *www.ethnicgrocer.com*.

FOR THE RUB:

¼ **cup sweet Spanish paprika**

1 **tablespoon ground cumin**

1 **tablespoon dry mustard**

1 **tablespoon ground fennel seeds**

2 **teaspoons salt**

2 **teaspoons coarsely ground black pepper**

Combine all the ingredients in a small bowl or jar with a tight-fitting lid. *(The rub keeps well for months stored at room temperature in a jar with a tight-fitting lid.)*

FOR THE GLAZE:

1 **cup pomegranate molasses (see headnote)**

½ **cup prepared horseradish, drained**

1 **tablespoon Dijon mustard**

1 **teaspoon coarsely ground black pepper**

½ **teaspoon salt**

Whisk together all the ingredients in a bowl. *(The glaze can be made a few days in advance, covered, and kept refrigerated. Bring to room temperature before using.)*

FOR THE CHICKEN:
2 (3-pound) chickens, butterflied (page 178)
2 tablespoons olive oil

CHICKEN,
DUCK,
AND
OTHER
BIRDS

177

1. Heat your grill to medium (page 3). Set aside a few tablespoons of glaze for brushing the cooked chicken.

2. Rub the chickens all over with the spice rub. Drizzle the chickens with oil and place skin side down on the grate. Grill, without moving the chicken, until the skin forms a crust and pulls away from the grate, 10 to 12 minutes. Turn the chickens over, close the grill hood, and grill until just cooked through (page 5), about 15 minutes more. During the last 5 minutes of cooking, brush the chicken often with glaze.

3. Remove the chicken to a cutting board and brush with the reserved glaze. Let rest for 5 minutes. Cut each chicken in half, using poultry shears or a heavy knife, and serve immediately.

Serves 4; can be doubled for 6 to 8 (no need to double the rub or the glaze)

Butterflied Chicken with Rosemary-Lemon-Garlic Oil, Parmesan, and Black Pepper

BOBBY
FLAY'S
BOY
GETS
GRILL

178

What could be more Italian or more savory than the combination of rosemary, garlic, lemon, and Parmigiano-Reggiano? Real Parmigiano—unlike most of the "Parmesan-style" grating cheeses—has a rich tanginess that makes it wonderful with the burn of black pepper. I put them all together to make this grilled chicken dish, a year-round favorite at my house; my pushy friends often demand it when they're coming to dinner!

"Butterflying" is the pretty name for removing the backbone of a chicken and flattening the breast so that the chicken lies flat and cooks evenly on the grill. Ask at the butcher counter to have someone do this for you.

1½ cups olive oil
6 cloves garlic, chopped
¼ cup chopped fresh rosemary leaves
Grated zest of 2 lemons
Salt and freshly ground black pepper
2 (3-pound) chickens, butterflied (see headnote)
½ cup freshly grated Parmigiano-
    Reggiano cheese
2 teaspoons coarsely ground black pepper

---

1. Combine the oil, garlic, rosemary, zest, and a sprinkling of salt and pepper in a blender and blend until smooth. Place the chickens in a large dish or a sealable plastic bag, pour half of the oil mixture over the chickens, and turn to coat. (Refrigerate the remaining marinade.) Cover the chickens and refrigerate for at least 4 hours and up to overnight. Remove from the refrigerator 30 minutes before cooking.

2. Heat your grill to medium (page 3).

3. Remove the chickens from the marinade and season with salt and pepper. Grill until the skin forms a crust and pulls away from the grate, 8 to 10 minutes. Turn the chickens

over, close the grill hood, and grill, basting with the reserved marinade until just cooked through (page 5), about 15 minutes more.

4. Remove the chickens to a cutting board and let rest for 10 minutes. Mix together the cheese and black pepper. Cut the chickens in half, and then in half again, using poultry shears or a heavy knife. Transfer to a platter or serving plates, sprinkle with the cheese mixture, and serve immediately.

Serves 4; can be doubled for 6 to 8 (no need to double the marinade)

Grilled Chicken in Adobo
with Garlic Butter

BOBBY
FLAY'S
BOY
GETS
GRILL

180

The word *adobo* describes a savory combination of salt, chile, and garlic that is used as a fundamental seasoning in many cuisines, from the Philippines to Cuba to Mexico, and in every Latin neighborhood in New York. No two adobos seem to be the same, but to anyone who grew up eating adobo, it is the taste of home. It's kind of like barbecue; you love the kind you grew up with, and people get really passionate about it. *Pollo adobado,* chicken cooked in adobo, is not too spicy but very flavorful, and easy to make for a big party.

6 dried New Mexico chiles, stemmed
and seeded
6 cloves garlic, chopped
¼ cup fresh lime juice
2 tablespoons chopped fresh oregano
leaves
1 tablespoon honey
Salt and freshly ground black pepper
2 (3-pound) chickens, quartered
Garlic butter (page 70)

1. Place the chiles in a bowl and cover with boiling water. Let sit until the chiles are soft and flexible, about 1 hour.

2. Drain the chiles and combine in a blender with 1 cup of the soaking liquid. Add the garlic, lime juice, oregano, and honey and blend until smooth. Season to taste with salt and pepper.

3. Place the chickens in a large dish, pour the marinade over them, and turn to coat. Cover and refrigerate for at least 2 hours and up to 4 hours. Remove from the refrigerator about 30 minutes before cooking.

4. Heat your grill to medium (page 3). Remove the chickens from the marinade and season all over with salt and pepper.

5. Grill, without moving the chicken, until the skin forms a crust and pulls away from the grate, 10 to 12 minutes. Turn the pieces over, close the grill hood, and grill until just cooked through, about 10 minutes more.

6. Remove the chickens from the grill, brush with the garlic butter, and let rest for 5 minutes before serving. Serve immediately.

Serves 4; can be doubled for 6 to 8 (no need to double the marinade or the butter)

Portuguese-Style Chicken
with Spicy Sausage and Mussels

BOBBY
FLAY'S
BOY
GETS
GRILL

182

Chicken, sausage, and mussels may sound like an odd combination, but just think of it as paella—without all the rice. A garlicky broth binds the ingredients together instead.

The fun thing about this dish is that you grill the ingredients separately, then stick a pot right on the grate of the grill and finish it that way. I find that my guests are really intrigued by this new grilling move.

Portuguese *chouriço* (like Spanish chorizo) is a hard, well-cured sausage, like Italian soppressata or pepperoni. It's different from Mexican-style chorizo, which is soft and fresh, like Italian sausage links. You want the hard kind for this recipe; if you can't find it in your neighborhood, order from *www.amarals.com*.

**1 (3- to 4-pound) chicken, cut into
    8 serving pieces**
5 tablespoons olive oil
2 tablespoons hot paprika
Salt and freshly ground black pepper
**1 pound Portuguese *chouriço* or Spanish
    chorizo (see headnote)**
1 large yellow onion, finely chopped
6 cloves garlic, finely chopped
2 cups dry white wine
1 pound cultivated mussels, scrubbed
1 cup homemade chicken stock or low-sodium canned chicken broth
2 tablespoons unsalted butter, cold
¼ cup chopped fresh flat-leaf parsley leaves

---

1. Heat your grill to medium (page 3).

2. Brush the chicken with 2 tablespoons of the oil and season all over with the paprika and salt and pepper. Put the chicken skin side down on the grate and grill until golden brown and lightly charred, 8 to 10 minutes. Turn the pieces over, reduce the heat to

medium or move to a cooler part of the grill, close the grill hood, and grill until cooked through (page 5), 4 to 5 minutes more for wings, 8 to 10 minutes more for breasts, 10 to 12 minutes more for legs and thighs. Remove the chicken to a plate and cover loosely with foil.

3. Grill the *chouriço* until browned on all sides, about 10 minutes total. Remove from the grill and cut into ½-inch pieces. Set aside.

4. Place a large pot on the grate of the grill (or on your stovetop) and add the remaining 3 tablespoons oil. Add the onion and garlic and cook, stirring, until soft, about 8 minutes; do not brown. Add the wine and simmer until reduced by half. Add the mussels and stock, cover the pot, and simmer until the mussels have opened, about 5 minutes (discard any mussels that do not open).

5. Remove the mussels to serving bowls with a slotted spoon. Put the chicken and *chouriço* in the pot and simmer for 3 minutes, until just heated through. Remove the chicken and *chouriço* to the serving bowls with a slotted spoon.

6. Without turning off the heat, quickly whisk the butter into the liquid in the pot until melted, season to taste with salt and pepper, and stir in the parsley. Ladle the hot liquid into the serving bowls. Serve immediately.

Serves 4

Herb-Rubbed Grilled Whole Turkey

Just wait until you tell your family that you'll be grilling the turkey this year, just for a change. Expect a lot of nervous questions and doubtful looks, all of which will disappear when you bring in the perfectly browned, deliciously smoky, perfectly cooked bird. And for once, you'll have enough room in the oven for all their side dishes. If you are feeding more people, grill two smaller turkeys rather than one larger one.

With this technique, you're getting your grill to act more like an oven, with what's called indirect heat. You want the heat to come from the bottom, sides, and top of the grill, instead of just the bottom (that's direct heat).

To do this on a gas grill, put a foil pan upside down over the ceramic briquets or whatever heat element your grill uses. In a kettle grill, put the pan over the coals in the center and also place a ring of coals around the edge of the pan. This will make for more even heat.

---

1 cup mild vegetable oil, such as canola

8 cloves garlic, coarsely chopped

½ cup finely chopped fresh flat-leaf parsley leaves

¼ cup chopped fresh tarragon leaves

¼ cup chopped fresh thyme leaves

¼ cup chopped fresh rosemary leaves

2 jalapeño chiles, seeded and coarsely chopped

2 tablespoons grated lime zest

2 tablespoons grated orange zest

1 tablespoon ancho chile powder

2 teaspoons kosher salt

2 teaspoons coarsely ground black pepper

1 (12-pound) fresh turkey, rinsed well and giblets removed

---

1. Combine the oil, garlic, parsley, tarragon, thyme, rosemary, jalapeño, lime zest, orange zest, ancho powder, salt, and pepper in a food processor or blender and process to a paste. Rub the paste over the entire turkey, including inside the cavity.

2. Heat your grill to high (page 3) and set up for indirect grilling (see headnote).

3. Place the turkey on the grill and reduce the heat to medium (if using charcoal, place the turkey on the cooler part of the grill). Close the grill hood.

4. Grill the turkey, without turning or basting, until an instant-read thermometer inserted into the thigh registers about 165 degrees F, about 3 hours. If you have a thermometer on your grill, try to keep it at about 350 degrees F. If using charcoal, add about 2 dozen coals every hour to maintain the heat.

5. Remove the turkey to a carving board and let rest for 20 minutes before carving.

Serves 8

CHICKEN,
DUCK,
AND
OTHER
BIRDS

Asian-Spiced Duck Breasts with Ginger-Chile Glaze

BOBBY
FLAY'S
BOY
GETS
GRILL

186

Asian chile pastes are great to keep on hand during grilling season; I have a collection that keeps growing, thanks to my frequent trips to Chinatown. (I can never resist a jar that has chiles in it.) Just chiles pounded with vinegar and sometimes garlic, pastes such as Thai sambal keep practically forever and give you a good base of sweet-hot flavor to work from when making sauces and marinades.

I love to serve duck breasts. They're luxurious and festive but really easy, and they cook better on the grill than anywhere else. All that delicious fat falls away from the meat as it cooks, leaving behind plenty of flavor. The leftover spice rub works well on any poultry or meat.

FOR THE RUB:

2 tablespoons Spanish paprika

1 tablespoon dry mustard

2 teaspoons salt

2 teaspoons freshly ground black pepper

2 teaspoons ground star anise

2 teaspoons ground ginger

1 teaspoon ground allspice

¼ teaspoon cayenne

Combine all the ingredients in a small bowl or jar with a tight-fitting lid. *(The rub keeps well for months stored at room temperature in a jar with a tight-fitting lid.)*

FOR THE GLAZE:

2 tablespoons peanut oil

1 (2-inch) piece fresh ginger, peeled and finely chopped

6 cloves garlic, finely chopped

2 tablespoons Asian red chile paste

½ cup honey
¼ cup soy sauce

Heat the oil in a small saucepan over medium-high heat. Add the ginger and garlic and cook, stirring, until softened, about 5 minutes; do not brown. Add the chile paste and cook, stirring, for 1 minute. Whisk in the honey and soy sauce and simmer for just a minute, until the honey has melted. Let cool to room temperature. *(The glaze can be made a few days in advance, covered, and kept refrigerated. Bring to room temperature before using.)*

FOR THE DUCK:

4 (6- to 8-ounce) skin-on, boneless
    duck breast halves
Salt and freshly ground black pepper
Thinly sliced scallions

1. Heat your grill to medium (page 3). Set aside a few tablespoons of the glaze for brushing the cooked duck.

2. Using the tip of a sharp knife, score the skin of the duck breasts in a crisscross pattern, being sure not to cut through to the flesh. Season with salt and pepper. Rub the skin side of each breast with a few teaspoons of the spice rub.

3. Put the breasts skin side down on the grate (use the cooler part of the grill if cooking with charcoal) and grill until the skin begins to crisp, 6 to 8 minutes. Turn the breasts over, raise the heat to high or move to the hotter part of the grill, brush with the glaze, and grill, brushing often with the glaze, until medium-rare (page 5), 3 to 4 minutes more.

4. Remove the breasts from the grill and brush with the reserved glaze. Let rest for 5 minutes, then cut each breast into ½-inch-thick slices. Serve immediately, sprinkled with scallions.

Serves 4; can be doubled for 6 to 8 (no need to double the rub or the glaze)

Peking Duck Breasts with Scallions, Pancakes, and Grilled Oranges

Peking duck has to be my favorite Chinese dish of all time. I've always loved duck, and when it's glazed with spice and honey and rolled up with bittersweet hoisin sauce, crunchy fresh scallion and cucumber, and pillowy pancakes, I think I could eat an entire bird by myself.

You probably never thought you could make it at home—it didn't occur to me for a long time—but you can, easily. This version is quick, delicious, and made with just breasts, which are much easier to cook, slice, and serve.

FOR THE GLAZE:

2 tablespoons peanut oil

1 medium white onion, coarsely chopped

3 cloves garlic, coarsely chopped

1 (1-inch) piece fresh ginger, peeled
    and coarsely chopped

2 cups diced canned plum
    tomatoes

½ cup water

1 cup hoisin sauce

¼ cup ketchup

3 tablespoons soy sauce

3 tablespoons rice vinegar

2 tablespoons honey

1 tablespoon Asian red chile paste,
    such as sambal

Salt and freshly ground black pepper

1. Heat the oil in a medium saucepan over medium-high heat. Add the onion, garlic, and ginger and cook, stirring, until soft, about 8 minutes; do not brown. Add the remaining ingredients, season to taste with salt and pepper, and simmer for 20 minutes.

2. Transfer the mixture to a blender and blend until smooth, or use a handheld blender and blend it in the pot. Return to the pot and simmer again until thickened, 15 to 20 min-

utes. Let cool to room temperature. *(The glaze can be made a few days in advance, covered, and kept refrigerated. Bring to room temperature before using.)*

CHICKEN,
DUCK,
AND
OTHER
BIRDS

189

FOR THE DUCK:

4 (6- to 8-ounce) skin-on, boneless duck
    breast halves
Salt and freshly ground black pepper
2 oranges, halved
12 to 16 plain Chinese pancakes (available
    at Asian grocers) or 6-inch flour tortillas
6 to 8 scallions, cut into 3-inch lengths,
    soaked in ice water, and drained

1. Heat your grill to medium (page 3). Set aside 2 tablespoons of the glaze for brushing the cooked duck and about 1 cup of the glaze for serving.

2. Using a knife, score the skin of each duck breast in a crisscross pattern, being careful not to cut through the fat to the flesh. Season with salt and pepper.

3. Put the breasts skin side down on the grate (use the cooler part of the grill if cooking with charcoal) and grill until the skin begins to crisp, 6 to 8 minutes. Turn the breasts over, raise the heat to high or move to the hotter part of the grill, brush with the glaze, and grill, brushing often with the glaze, until medium-rare (page 5), 3 to 4 minutes more.

4. Remove the breasts from the grill (leave the grill on) and brush with the reserved 2 tablespoons glaze. Let rest for 5 minutes, then cut each breast into ½-inch-thick slices.

5. Meanwhile place the oranges cut side down on the grate and grill until lightly charred, 3 to 5 minutes. Wrap the pancakes together in foil and place on the grill to warm, 3 to 5 minutes. Remove the oranges from the grill and cut each orange half into wedges.

6. Serve the duck immediately on a platter surrounded by the orange wedges. Pass the remaining glaze, the scallions, and pancakes. To eat, spread some hoisin glaze on a pancake, add a few slices of duck, top with a scallion, squeeze grilled orange over the meat, fold, and eat.

Serves 4; can be doubled for 6 to 8 (no need to double the glaze)

Roast Duck with Sweet–Hot Mustard–Mint Glaze

I've borrowed part of the classic method for Chinese roast duck for this recipe. No, not the part where you blow the duck up with a bicycle pump to separate the skin from the meat, or the part where you carve the duck into exactly 120 pieces for serving. But I do leave my ducks uncovered in the refrigerator for a day, which dries out the skin somewhat. This makes a huge difference to the finished dish—the skin gets incredibly crisp.

You'll need a rotisserie attachment to make this recipe. If you don't have one but you like the sound of the glaze, go ahead and use it in the duck breast recipe on page 186, instead of the ginger-chile glaze.

**1 (5- to 6-pound) whole duck,
    preferably fresh**
6 tablespoons Dijon mustard
3 tablespoons honey
**2 tablespoons prepared horseradish,
    drained**
8 fresh mint leaves, finely chopped
Salt and freshly ground black pepper

---

1. One day before serving, place the duck on a wire rack set over a rimmed baking sheet and refrigerate uncovered.

2. Whisk the mustard, honey, horseradish, and mint together in a small bowl and season to taste with salt and pepper. *(The glaze can be made a few days in advance, covered, and kept refrigerated. Bring to room temperature before using.)*

3. Heat your grill to medium (page 3) and set up the rotisserie attachment. Put a foil pan in the bottom of the grill to catch the fat. If using a charcoal grill, put the pan directly under the duck and move the coals to the sides of the grill.

4. Set aside a few tablespoons of the glaze for brushing the duck after it's cooked. Season the duck all over with salt and pepper.

5. Skewer the duck onto the rotisserie rod. Start the rotisserie and cook until the skin is crisp and the breast meat is cooked through and tender, 50 to 60 minutes (the internal temperature should be about 175 degrees F on an instant-read thermometer).

6. During the last 20 minutes of cooking, brush with the glaze every 5 minutes. Remove from the grill and brush with the reserved glaze. Let rest for 10 minutes before carving.

Serves 4 to 6

Grilled Black and White Pepper Quail

BOBBY
FLAY'S
BOY
GETS
GRILL

192

Grilling is a simple way to experiment with cooking game birds. Small quail are fun to eat—just use your hands—and the meat is pleasantly rich, with more flavor than chicken. They are usually sold "partially boned" and are very easy to grill. If you live in the South or West, you may be able to hunt your own quail (I have friends in Texas who do just that), or you can order yours from *www.dartagnan.com*.

Serve this with a big, hearty salad, like Grilled Potato Salad with Watercress, Scallions, and Blue Cheese Vinaigrette (page 84), or for a real feast, as an additional entrée next to a grilled steak.

FOR THE GLAZE:

¼ **cup pure maple syrup**

2 cups pineapple juice

Combine the syrup and juice in a small saucepan (not aluminum or cast-iron) and simmer until reduced by half, about 15 minutes. *(The glaze can be made a few days in advance, covered, and kept refrigerated. Bring to room temperature before using.)*

FOR THE QUAIL:

1 tablespoon ground white pepper

1 tablespoon freshly ground black pepper

1 tablespoon salt

8 partially boned quail

2 tablespoons olive oil

1. Heat your grill to high (page 3).

2. Combine the white and black peppers and salt in a small bowl. Brush the quail with oil on both sides and season with some of the pepper mixture.

3. Grill for 2 to 3 minutes on each side, brushing often with the glaze, until the skin is crisp and glazed and the meat is firm and just cooked through (page 5).

4. Remove from the grill and sprinkle with more of the pepper mixture. Serve immediately.

Serves 4; can be doubled for 6 to 8 (no need to double the glaze)

Tandoori-Marinated Rotisserie Cornish Hens

Yogurt marinades are India's great contribution to grilling. Yogurt has tenderizing qualities that give chicken a velvety texture. It also helps the spices permeate the meat so that you can actually taste them—not always the case with marinades, whose flavors often disappear after grilling. And the spicy yogurt marinade caramelizes as it cooks, creating a crust that's sticky in the best way, like barbecued ribs.

You will need a rotisserie attachment to make this recipe, but the marinade is also excellent for chicken pieces and lamb chops.

Tandoori marinade (page 98)
4 (2- to 2½-pound) Cornish hens
1 medium white onion
Fresh cilantro sprigs
Lime wedges

1. Combine the marinade and the hens in a glass or plastic dish. Rub the marinade all over the hens, including the cavities. Cover and refrigerate for at least 4 hours and up to 24 hours.

2. Heat your grill to high (page 3) and set up the rotisserie attachment.

3. Skewer the hens on the rotisserie rod. Start the rotisserie and cook until golden and cooked through (the internal temperature should be about 175 degrees F on an instant-read thermometer), about 45 minutes.

4. While the hens are grilling, slice the onion into thin rings, place them in a bowl of ice water, cover, and refrigerate. Right before serving, remove the onion from the water and pat dry.

5. Cut the hens in half (if desired) and serve with onion slices, cilantro sprigs, and lime wedges.

Serves 4; can be doubled for 6 to 8 (no need to double the marinade)

Crispy Capon Breast
with Cuban Barbecue Sauce

Capon breast (like turkey breast) is a great way to feed a lot of people those nice, clean breast slices they always seem to want! But breast meat doesn't have to be plain; this has a crisp skin with a spicy, orange-spiked glaze, and juicy meat from an overnight brining process that both tenderizes and flavors.

Capons are large, castrated male chickens (they're older than roasters and fryers) that weigh about 8 pounds and are mostly breast. You can order bone-in capon breast from *www.eberlypoultry.com*, where all the poultry is organically raised, free-range—and delicious. You could also substitute a small turkey breast.

FOR THE CAPON:

2½ **quarts cold water**

1 **cup kosher salt**

12 **black peppercorns**

1 **(3- to 4-pound) bone-in capon breast**
    (see headnote)

The day before serving, mix the water and salt in a large bowl until dissolved. Add the peppercorns and capon, cover, and refrigerate for 24 hours, turning occasionally.

FOR THE SAUCE:

2 **cups orange juice**

1 **cup red wine vinegar**

1 **cup white wine vinegar**

3 **cups granulated sugar**

Grated zest of 1 orange

3 **tablespoons mild vegetable oil,**
    such as canola

1 **large yellow onion, coarsely chopped**

1 **head garlic, cloves peeled**
    and coarsely chopped

1 habanero chile, seeded
   and coarsely chopped
3 cups canned plum tomatoes
   with their juices, chopped
¼ cup ketchup
¼ cup molasses
3 tablespoons ancho chile powder
2 tablespoons dark brown sugar
2 tablespoons honey
2 tablespoons Dijon mustard
1 tablespoon Worcestershire sauce
2 teaspoons chipotle purée (page 12)
Salt and freshly ground black pepper

1. Combine the orange juice, vinegars, and granulated sugar in a medium saucepan (not aluminum or cast-iron) and boil until reduced to about 1 cup. Remove from the heat, stir in the orange zest, and set aside.

2. In another saucepan, heat the oil over medium-high heat. Add the onion, garlic, and habanero and cook, stirring, until soft, about 5 minutes; do not brown. Add the remaining ingredients and simmer until the tomatoes are soft and the sauce has thickened, about 40 minutes.

3. Transfer the mixture to a blender or food processor and process until smooth. Season to taste with salt and pepper and return to the pot. Bring to a simmer and whisk in the orange mixture. Simmer for 10 minutes and set aside to cool. *(The sauce can be made a few days in advance, covered, and kept refrigerated. Bring to room temperature before using.)*

TO SERVE:
Freshly ground black pepper

1. Heat your grill to medium (page 3). Set aside a few tablespoons of sauce for brushing the cooked capon.

2. Remove the capon from the brine, pat dry, and season it all over with pepper.

3. Place the capon breast skin side down on the grate and grill until golden brown and the skin pulls away from the grate, 10 to 12 minutes. Turn the breast over and grill until just cooked through, 8 to 10 minutes more, basting with the sauce every few minutes.

4. Remove the breast from the grill and brush with the reserved sauce. Let rest for 5 minutes before slicing. Serve immediately.

Serves 6 to 8

BEEF, LAMB, PORK, AND SAUSAGES

Pressed Cuban-Style Burger

**BOBBY
FLAY'S
BOY
GETS
GRILL**

198

When I'm really, really hungry, all I think about is a big, fat burger oozing melted cheese and pickles. Unless I'm in Miami, when all I think about is a big, fat Cuban sandwich oozing melted cheese and pickles. Cheeseburgers and Cuban sandwiches are my two favorite indulgences, and they're actually pretty similar. This sandwich combines the two.

Don't be tempted to use fancy crusty bread here. Only soft rolls will get the perfect crisp crust you want to play against the soft interior. As for the meat, chuck is about 80 percent lean, which grinds to the right texture for burgers. Note that you'll need a heavy pot or a couple of bricks to press the burgers.

**1 pound freshly ground beef,
    preferably chuck (see headnote)
Salt and freshly ground black pepper
½ cup mayonnaise
3 cloves garlic, roasted (page 9)
    and puréed
4 hamburger buns
2 to 3 tablespoons Dijon mustard
8 thin slices Swiss cheese
4 thin slices ham
2 dill pickles, cut into ¼-inch-thick slices
    (about 16)**

1. Heat your grill to high (page 3).

2. Form the meat into four burgers. Season all over with salt and pepper. Grill the burgers until medium-rare (page 5), about 3 minutes on each side. Remove from the grill and leave the grill on.

3. Combine the mayonnaise and roasted garlic in a small bowl and season to taste with salt and pepper. Spread the cut sides of each bun with garlic mayonnaise and mustard. Place a slice of cheese on the bottom of each bun and a burger on top of the cheese, then top the burger with a slice of ham. Add another slice of cheese, then the pickle slices.

Cover with the tops of the buns and wrap each burger individually in aluminum foil.

4. Place the burgers close together on the grill and rest a heavy skillet or a couple of bricks on top of them, pressing down if needed to flatten them. Grill for 2 to 3 minutes until the cheese is melted. Serve immediately.

Serves 4; can be doubled for 6 to 8

Black Pepper–Ancho–Crusted Beef Filets with Hot-and-Sweet Mint Glaze

Ancho chiles, black pepper, fresh mint, even a little horseradish—there are plenty of bold flavors here, giving a lift to tender, buttery filet mignon. Serve this dish with Maple-Glazed Grilled Sweet Potatoes (page 86).

I always buy 8 ounces of steak per person, though some cookbooks recommend just 4 ounces or so. In my experience, people who like steak can really put it away. (Including me.) And if you make too much, what's the worst that could happen? Leftovers! This tender filet, with its peppery crust and spicy glaze, makes amazing steak sandwiches the day after.

FOR THE GLAZE:

6 tablespoons Dijon mustard

¼ cup honey

2 tablespoons prepared horseradish, drained

6 fresh mint leaves, finely chopped

Salt and freshly ground black pepper

Whisk together the mustard, honey, horseradish, and mint in a small bowl and season with salt and pepper to taste. Set aside at room temperature. *(The glaze can be made a few days in advance, covered, and kept refrigerated. Bring to room temperature before using.)*

FOR THE FILETS:

2 tablespoons coarsely ground black pepper

1 tablespoon ancho chile powder

1 tablespoon salt

4 (8-ounce) filets mignons

2 tablespoons mild vegetable oil,
    such as canola

1. Heat your grill to high (page 3).

2. Combine the pepper, ancho powder, and salt in a small bowl. Rub each filet on one side with the spice mixture and drizzle with the oil. Set aside a few tablespoons of glaze to brush on the cooked filets.

3. Grill the filets spiced side down until the bottom is lightly charred and crusty, about 4 minutes. Turn the filets over, reduce the heat to medium or move to a cooler part of the grill, and brush the top with the glaze. Grill, brushing often with the glaze, until medium-rare (page 5), about 4 minutes more.

4. Remove the filets to a cutting board and brush with the reserved glaze. Let rest 5 minutes before serving.

Serves 4; can be doubled for 6 to 8

Steak Salad with Watercress, Blue Cheese, and Cherry Tomato–Hot Sauce Dressing

After a hot summer weekend of grilling, my favorite Sunday dinner is a cool steak salad with all my favorite sides tossed into the bowl: tomatoes, watercress, blue cheese, and red onions. If I don't have leftover steak (which also works really well in this recipe), I cook up a few filets mignons—their tenderness works perfectly in a salad. The cumin and garlic cook into a fabulous, almost spicy crust for the meat.

FOR THE DRESSING:

¼ **cup red wine vinegar**

1 **tablespoon Dijon mustard**

2 **teaspoons chipotle purée (page 12)**

1 **tablespoon honey**

Salt and freshly ground black pepper

½ **cup mild vegetable oil, such as canola**

1 **cup cherry or grape tomatoes, cut in half**

3 **tablespoons chopped fresh cilantro leaves**

Whisk together the vinegar, mustard, chipotle purée, and honey in a medium bowl. Season to taste with salt and pepper. Gradually whisk in the oil until emulsified. Fold in the tomatoes and cilantro and let sit at room temperature for 30 minutes. *(The dressing can be made a few hours in advance, covered, and kept refrigerated. Bring to room temperature before serving.)*

FOR THE FILETS:

½ **cup olive oil**

10 **cloves garlic, finely chopped**

2 **tablespoons ground cumin**

2 **teaspoons salt**

1 **teaspoon freshly ground black pepper**

4 **(8-ounce) filets mignons**

1. Heat your grill to high (page 3).

2. Combine the olive oil, garlic, cumin, salt, and pepper in a small bowl and mix to form a paste. Rub each steak on one side with the mixture.

3. Grill the filets garlic side down until crusty and golden brown, 3 to 4 minutes, being careful not to let the garlic burn. Turn the filets over, reduce the heat to medium or move to a cooler part of the grill, and grill until medium-rare (page 5), 5 to 6 minutes more.

4. Remove the filets from the grill and let rest for 5 minutes. Cut into ½-inch-thick slices and set aside at room temperature. *(The steaks can be cooked, covered—do not slice— and set aside at room temperature up to 1 hour in advance, or refrigerated overnight. Bring to room temperature and slice just before serving.)*

FOR THE SALAD:
4 large handfuls watercress
8 ounces blue cheese, preferably goat's milk,
   crumbled
½ red onion, thinly sliced
Fresh cilantro leaves

Divide the watercress, cheese, and onion among 4 large plates. Divide the sliced meat on top and spoon tomatoes and a few tablespoons of the dressing over the top. Garnish with cilantro. Serve immediately.

Serves 4; can be doubled for 6 to 8 (no need to double the dressing)

Black Pepper–Crusted Strip Steaks with Mint Chimichurri

Chimichurri, a pungent steak sauce of olive oil, garlic, and parsley, is Argentina's greatest contribution to world grilling. Every Argentine *churrascaría* (steakhouse) in New York has bowls of chimichurri on the table—and I've been known to eat an entire bowl by myself! I can't resist dipping crusty bread into it, and even the roasted potatoes that come with my steak.

I especially like the freshness of mint with steak, so I added a few handfuls to my chimichurri recipe. Strip steaks (also called shell steaks or club steaks) are great, relatively inexpensive cuts. They're sliced from the same top loin as the porterhouse but without the tenderloin attached.

FOR THE CHIMICHURRI:

2 cups fresh mint leaves

1 cup fresh flat-leaf parsley leaves

1 cup fresh cilantro leaves

8 cloves garlic, chopped

3 serrano chiles, roasted and seeded (page 9)

3 tablespoons honey

3 tablespoons Dijon mustard

1 cup olive oil

Salt and freshly ground black pepper

Combine the mint, parsley, cilantro, garlic, chiles, honey, and mustard in a food processor or blender and process to a paste. With the motor running, slowly add the olive oil until emulsified. Transfer the mixture to a bowl. If the mixture is too thick, whisk in a few tablespoons of cold water to loosen it (the sauce should be like a chunky vinaigrette, not like a mayonnaise). Season to taste with salt and pepper. *(The chimichurri can be made a few hours in advance and set aside at room temperature.)*

4 (12-ounce) strip or shell steaks

Kosher salt

Coarsely cracked black pepper

1. Heat your grill to high (page 3).

2. Season the steaks with plenty of salt and pepper. Grill until lightly charred and crusty, 3 to 4 minutes. Turn the steaks over, reduce the heat to medium or move to a cooler part of the grill, and cook until medium-rare (page 5), 5 to 6 minutes more.

3. Remove the steaks from the grill and let rest for 5 minutes. Cut into 1-inch-thick slices and serve immediately, spooning chimichurri over each serving.

Serves 6

BEEF, LAMB, PORK, AND SAUSAGES

205

Porterhouse Steaks
with Fra Diavolo Barbecue Sauce
and Cherry Pepper Salad

**BOBBY
FLAY'S
BOY
GETS
GRILL**

206

I came up with this Italian-American steak dish for the firemen who work in the Arthur Avenue neighborhood of the Bronx. It was an honor to cook for them (like most firemen, they really appreciate good food), and I wanted to grill them something special that would have a taste of their neighborhood, a real old-time Little Italy. Arthur Avenue is lined with stores that make fresh mozzarella, pasta, focaccia, and salami.

The porterhouse steaks should be cut very thick, so that they turn out crusty on the outside and red-rare inside. (In Italy, the porterhouse cut, called *tagliata,* is always cut and cooked this way.) For the sauce, I decided to introduce my favorite red sauce—a spicy, garlicky fra diavolo—to a smoky-sweet American barbecue sauce. And the savory relish of tomatoes, roasted peppers, and parsley completes the dish. Serve it with plain spaghetti or crusty bread, and you have a seriously good dinner.

FOR THE SAUCE:

3 tablespoons olive oil

1 Spanish onion, finely chopped

4 cloves garlic, finely chopped

1 tablespoon hot red pepper flakes

3 cups canned plum tomatoes, puréed

1 cup dark brown sugar

2 tablespoons tomato paste

2 tablespoons honey

2 tablespoons chopped fresh flat-leaf
   parsley leaves

2 tablespoons chopped fresh
   basil leaves

1 tablespoon chopped fresh
   oregano leaves

Salt and freshly ground black pepper

Heat the oil in a saucepan over medium-high heat, add the onion, and cook, stirring until soft, about 5 minutes; do not brown. Add the garlic and pepper flakes and cook for 1 minute. Add the remaining ingredients, season to taste with salt and pepper, and simmer until thickened, 35 to 40 minutes. *(The sauce can be made 2 days in advance, cooled, covered, and kept refrigerated. Bring to room temperature before serving.)*

FOR THE SALAD:

¼ **cup red wine vinegar**

1 **clove garlic, finely chopped**

½ **cup olive oil**

Salt and freshly ground black pepper

8 **ounces cherry peppers, unpeeled, or 1 large red bell pepper, roasted, peeled, seeded (page 9), and diced**

1 **cup cherry or grape tomatoes, cut in half**

¼ **cup chopped fresh flat-leaf parsley leaves**

Whisk together the vinegar and garlic in a medium bowl. Gradually whisk in the olive oil and season to taste with salt and pepper. Add the peppers, tomatoes, and parsley and stir to combine. Taste for salt and pepper and set aside at room temperature. *(The salad can be made a few hours in advance, covered, and kept refrigerated. Bring to room temperature before serving.)*

FOR THE STEAKS:

2 **(28-ounce) bone-in porterhouse steaks, about 1½ inches thick**

Salt and freshly ground black pepper

1. Heat your grill to high (page 3).

2. Season the steaks with plenty of salt and pepper. Set aside a few tablespoons of sauce for brushing on the cooked steaks and set aside about ½ cup of sauce to pass at the table.

3. Grill the steaks until lightly charred and crusty, 4 to 5 minutes. Turn the steaks over, reduce the heat to medium or move to a cooler part of the grill, and brush the tops of the steaks with sauce. Close the grill hood and grill for 5 minutes.

4. Open the grill hood and continue grilling, brushing often with the sauce, until medium-rare (page 5), about 5 minutes more.

5. Remove the meat from the grill and brush with the reserved sauce. Let rest for 5 minutes, then cut into 1-inch-thick slices. Top with the tomato salad and serve immediately. Pass the sauce on the side.

Serves 4; can be doubled for 6 to 8 (no need to double the sauce)

BEEF,
LAMB,
PORK,
AND
SAUSAGES

209

Barbecued Brisket Sandwiches on Texas Toast

BOBBY
FLAY'S
BOY
GETS
GRILL

210

Like this barbecued brisket, my girlfriend, Stephanie, is a spicy, irresistible, and authentic Texan. She gave me some tips on the recipe, like serving it with Texas toast: thick slices of grilled bread that soak up all the amazing juices from the meat. (Texas barbecue purists don't believe in barbecue sauce.) Yes, this recipe takes a while, but it's so worth it. Make it on a Sunday afternoon in football season—you'll catch all the games that way.

Authentic barbecue is easy to make with the inexpensive home smokers available everywhere these days. I have a very basic charcoal smoker, and it worked great the first time I tried this legendary recipe. Even if you only have a regular charcoal kettle grill or a gas one, you can rig up almost any kind of grill to act as a smoker. Check the manual for your grill. Make sure that you can track the temperature inside the smoker—that's the trick to making great barbecue. The heat is actually more important than the smoke.

FOR THE MOP:

1 large red onion, chopped

4 cloves garlic, chopped

2 serrano chiles, chopped

6 (12-ounce) bottles dark beer

1 cup cider vinegar

½ cup dark brown sugar

2 bay leaves

Salt and freshly ground black pepper

Combine all the ingredients in a medium saucepan, season with salt and pepper, and simmer for 15 minutes. Remove from the heat and let cool slightly. (*The mop can be made a few days in advance, covered, and kept refrigerated.*)

FOR THE BRISKET:

¼ cup ancho chile powder

2 tablespoons sweet paprika

1 tablespoon ground cumin

1 tablespoon dry mustard

1 tablespoon salt

2 teaspoons cayenne

1 (5- to 6-pound) beef brisket, with a layer
of fat at least ¼ inch thick

6 cups wood chips, soaked in cold water
for 1 to 2 hours

BEEF,
LAMB,
PORK,
AND
SAUSAGES

211

1. Mix together the spices in a small bowl. Rub the entire brisket with the spice mixture, place it on a rimmed baking sheet, cover, and refrigerate for at least 1 hour and up to 6 hours.

2. Prepare the grill or smoker with about 1 cup soaked wood chips, and if using a charcoal grill, a chimney starter full of hot coals, according to the manufacturer's directions (see headnote). Heat to 180 to 200 degrees F.

3. Place the brisket fat side up in the grill or smoker, close the grill hood, and smoke, basting with the mop every 30 minutes. When you open the grill to baste, check the temperature inside; it should hover around 200 degrees. Every hour or so, add a cup of soaked wood chips to maintain the smoke, and if using a charcoal grill, about 2 dozen coals to fuel the fire. Smoke until the brisket is extremely tender and the internal temperature is about 145 degrees F, 5 to 6 hours.

4. Remove the meat from the grill and let rest for 10 minutes. Thinly slice the meat against the grain.

FOR THE TOAST:

16 tablespoons (2 sticks) unsalted butter,
at room temperature

8 cloves garlic, finely chopped

Salt and freshly ground black pepper

2 Pullman loaves white bread (or any good
white bread), cut into 1-inch-thick slices

1. Heat your grill to medium-high (page 3).

2. Mix together the butter and garlic in a bowl and season to taste with salt and pepper. Brush both sides of the bread with the butter.

3. Grill the bread on both sides until light golden brown, 1 to 2 minutes on each side.

4. Serve the sliced brisket piled on top of the toast.

Serves 6 (can be doubled for 10 to 12)

Balsamic-Marinated Flank Steak with Arugula, Tomato, and Shaved Parmesan Salad

BOBBY
FLAY'S
BOY
GETS
GRILL

214

In France your *steak frites* is always served with watercress; in Italy, your *tagliata* comes with arugula. As you cut the steak, the juices pour out and create a delicious dressing for the greens. This recipe expands on that idea with cherry tomatoes, shavings of sharp, nutty Parmigiano, and slivers of red onion, making a one-dish meal with slices of grilled crusty bread.

½ **cup plus 2 tablespoons balsamic vinegar**
¾ **cup plus 3 tablespoons olive oil**
4 **cloves garlic, coarsely chopped**
2 **tablespoons coarsely chopped rosemary leaves**
1 (1½- **to** 1¾-**pound) beef flank steak**
Salt and freshly ground black pepper
2 **cups arugula**
1 **pound cherry tomatoes, halved**
½ **small red onion, thinly sliced**
1 (4-**ounce) piece Parmesan cheese**

1. Whisk together ½ cup of the vinegar, ¾ cup of the oil, the garlic, and rosemary in a large dish (or use a thick, sealable plastic bag). Add the steak and turn to coat. Cover and let marinate in the refrigerator for at least 4 hours and up to 8 hours, turning every 2 hours.

2. Heat your grill to high (page 3).

3. Remove the steak from the marinade and season with salt and pepper. Grill until lightly charred and crusty, 4 to 5 minutes. Turn the steak over, reduce the heat to medium or move to a cooler part of the grill, and grill until medium-rare (page 5), 3 to 4 minutes more.

4. Remove the steak to a cutting board and let rest for 5 minutes. Cut into ½-inch-thick slices against the grain of the meat.

5. Whisk together the remaining 2 tablespoons vinegar and 3 tablespoons oil in a large bowl and season with salt and pepper. Add the arugula, tomatoes, and onion and toss to coat. Divide the sliced steak among 4 plates and top with some of the arugula salad. Using a vegetable peeler, shave thin slices of Parmesan over each dish. Serve immediately.

Serves 4; can be doubled for 6 to 8 (no need to double the marinade)

Coffee Spice–Rubbed Ribeye
with Smoky Tomato–Red Chile Salsa

BOBBY
FLAY'S
BOY
GETS
GRILL

216

Roasted coffee beans can be just as intense and flavor packed as the fresh spices I use in barbecue rubs, like cumin and peppercorns. Ground with a whole pack of spices, coffee adds richness and a toasty bitterness to this rub, my new favorite for beef and lamb. And roasted coffee and smoky chipotle together have as much jolt as a double espresso.

Texas toast is buttery, thick-sliced toast that's served—not just in Texas, but around the Southwest—with barbecue, steak, and any dish with tasty juices that need sopping up.

FOR THE RUB:

¼ cup ancho chile powder

¼ cup finely ground espresso-roast
      coffee beans

2 tablespoons sweet paprika

2 tablespoons dark brown sugar

1 tablespoon dry mustard

1 tablespoon salt

1 tablespoon freshly ground black pepper

1 tablespoon dried oregano

1 tablespoon ground coriander

2 teaspoons ground ginger

2 teaspoons chile de árbol powder (page 10)

Combine all the ingredients in a bowl or a jar with a tight-fitting lid and mix well. *(The rub keeps well for months stored at room temperature in a jar with a tight-fitting lid.)*

FOR THE SALSA:

¼ cup red wine vinegar

¼ cup olive oil

2 teaspoons chipotle purée (page 12)

3 ripe large tomatoes, diced

1 small red onion, halved and thinly sliced

1 serrano chile, seeded and finely chopped

¼ cup chopped fresh cilantro leaves

2 teaspoons honey

Salt and freshly ground black pepper

Whisk together the vinegar, oil, and chipotle purée in a medium bowl. Add the remaining ingredients and toss to combine. Season to taste with salt and pepper. *(The relish can be made a few hours in advance, covered, and kept refrigerated. Bring to room temperature before serving.)*

FOR THE STEAKS:

2 (24-ounce) bone-in or (20-ounce) boneless
    ribeye steaks, cut 2 inches thick

Salt and coarsely ground black pepper

½ recipe Texas toast (page 211)

1. Heat your grill to high (page 3).

2. Season the steaks with salt and pepper. Rub 2 tablespoons of the coffee rub onto one side of each steak. Grill the steaks rub side down, until lightly charred and crusty, 4 to 5 minutes. Turn the steaks over, reduce the heat to medium or move to a cooler part of the grill, close the grill hood, and grill until medium-rare (page 5), 8 to 10 minutes more.

3. Remove the steaks from the grill and let rest for 5 minutes. Lower the grill heat to medium-high (page 3) and prepare the Texas toast.

4. Cut the steaks into 1-inch-thick slices and serve immediately, topped with tomato salsa. Pass the toast on the side.

Serves 4; can be doubled for 6 to 8 (no need to double the rub)

Thick-Cut Ribeye
with Red Wine–Honey Mustard Vinaigrette
and Fresh Thyme

**BOBBY
FLAY'S
BOY
GETS
GRILL**

218

When you're cooking really good beef—and I strongly recommend buying Prime meat whenever you can; it just tastes so much better—a thick cut makes all the difference. I consider 2 inches the optimal thickness for a ribeye. You get to taste the charred crust, the rich, tender, blood-rare center, and all the flavor variations in between.

Boneless ribeye is the same piece of meat as prime rib but with the bone removed. I'd serve this fabulous steak with Parmesan-Crusted Portobello Mushroom Caps (page 69), plus a salad or Grilled Zucchini with Romesco Sauce and Hazelnuts (page 74).

FOR THE VINAIGRETTE:
¼ cup red wine vinegar
2 tablespoons Dijon mustard
1 tablespoon honey
1 tablespoon finely chopped fresh thyme leaves
Salt and freshly ground black pepper
¾ cup extra-virgin olive oil

Whisk together the vinegar, mustard, honey, and thyme in a medium bowl and season to taste with salt and pepper. Gradually whisk in the olive oil until emulsified. *(The vinaigrette can be made a few hours in advance, covered, and kept refrigerated. Bring to room temperature before serving.)*

FOR THE STEAKS:
2 (16-ounce) boneless ribeye steaks,
    cut 2 inches thick
Salt and freshly ground black pepper

1. Heat your grill to high (page 3).

2. Season the steaks with salt and pepper. Grill until lightly charred and crusty, 4 to 5 minutes. Turn the steaks over, reduce the heat to medium or move them to a cooler part of the grill, close the grill hood, and grill until medium-rare (page 5), 8 to 10 minutes more.

3. Remove the steaks to a cutting board and let rest for 5 minutes. Cut into ½-inch-thick slices, transfer to serving plates, and spoon a few tablespoons of the vinaigrette over each serving.

Serves 4; can be doubled for 6 to 8 (no need to double the dressing)

Grilled Ribeye Steak with Cilantro-Garlic Butter

The straightforward flavor punch of this dish made it my favorite steak recipe last summer. I was doing a lot of experimenting with flavored butters—as you can tell from the recipes in this book—and this is the one I kept pulling out of the freezer over and over again. Butter on steak is a French classic, but the way I do it, you're not watching a slice of frozen butter melt into a pool on your steak; instead, a brushing of soft butter mixes invisibly with the juices. It may be invisible, but the flavor is mind-blowing.

FOR THE BUTTER:

8 tablespoons (1 stick) unsalted butter,
   slightly softened
6 cloves garlic, coarsely chopped
¼ cup fresh cilantro leaves
1 to 2 teaspoons fresh lime juice
Salt and freshly ground black pepper

Combine the butter, garlic, cilantro, and 1 teaspoon lime juice in a food processor or with an electric mixer and process until smooth. (To do it by hand, finely chop the garlic and cilantro. Let the butter get very soft, then beat in the garlic, cilantro, and lime juice with a large wooden spoon.) Season to taste with salt, pepper, and additional lime juice if needed. *(The butter can be made in advance, wrapped, and kept refrigerated for 2 days, or frozen for a week. Bring to room temperature before using.)*

FOR THE STEAKS:

2 (16-ounce) boneless ribeye steaks,
   cut 2 inches thick
Salt and freshly ground black pepper

1. Heat your grill to high (page 3).

2. Season the steaks with salt and pepper. Grill until lightly charred and crusty, 4 to 5 minutes. Turn the steaks over, reduce the heat to medium or move to a cooler part of the grill, close the grill hood, and grill until medium-rare (page 5), 8 to 10 minutes longer.

3. Remove the steaks to a cutting board and brush liberally on both sides with the butter. Let rest for 5 minutes, then cut the steaks into 1-inch-thick slices and serve immediately.

Serves 4; can be doubled for 6 to 8 (no need to double the butter)

Smoky-Sweet Rotisserie Apricot-Chipotle-Glazed Lamb Tacos with Goat Cheese and Salsa Cruda

This dish will make you lots of new friends. Sounds like too much to promise, I know, but the roasting meat will make your entire neighborhood smell great for hours. With the sweetness of the apricot and chipotle glaze, the lamb tastes almost like it's been slow-barbecued—in a quarter of the time. It makes amazing tacos but is also great sliced and served with grilled corn and an avocado salad.

The apricots in the glaze will help form a sweet, smoky crust on the meat. However, the natural sugars will burn if left on the heat for too long—that's why you won't start glazing the meat until the end of the cooking time.

Note that you will need to use a rotisserie attachment to make the leg of lamb. You can use the same glaze for grilling lamb tenderloins.

FOR THE GLAZE:

2 tablespoons mild vegetable oil,
    such as canola
1 large red onion, coarsely chopped
2 cloves garlic, coarsely chopped
4 cups red wine vinegar
3 cups sugar
8 ounces dried apricots, soaked in warm
    water for 1 hour, drained, and chopped
1 tablespoon chipotle purée (page 12)
¼ cup chopped fresh cilantro leaves
Salt

1. Heat the oil in a medium-size saucepan (not aluminum or cast-iron) over medium-high heat. Add the onion and garlic and cook, stirring, until soft, about 8 minutes; do not brown. Add the vinegar and sugar, bring to a boil, and boil until reduced by half. Add the apricots and simmer for 10 minutes.

2. Transfer the mixture to a food processor or blender, add the chipotle purée and cilantro, and blend until smooth. Season to taste with salt and transfer to a bowl. *(The glaze can be made 1 day in advance, cooled, covered, and kept refrigerated. Bring to room temperature before using.)*

FOR THE SALSA:

6 ripe large tomatoes, cored, seeded
    and diced

½ red onion, diced

3 cloves garlic, chopped

1 jalapeño chile, seeded and minced

1 tablespoon Mexican oregano

¼ cup chopped fresh cilantro leaves

Juice of 1 lime

2 tablespoons mild vegetable oil,
    such as canola

2 teaspoons ancho chile powder

Salt and freshly ground black pepper

Combine all the ingredients in a bowl and let sit at room temperature for 30 minutes. *(The salsa can be made a few hours in advance, covered, and kept refrigerated. Bring to room temperature before serving.)*

FOR THE LAMB:

1 (7-pound) boneless leg of lamb, rolled
    and tied (someone at the butcher counter
    can do this for you)

Olive oil for brushing

Salt and and freshly ground black pepper

1 large red onion, sliced ½ inch thick

24 (6-inch) flour tortillas, stacked
    and wrapped in aluminum foil

1 pound fresh goat cheese, crumbled

3 hearts of romaine lettuce,
    sliced crosswise into shreds

---

1. Heat your grill to high (page 3) and set up the rotisserie attachment.

2. Brush the lamb with oil and season all over with salt and pepper. Place the lamb directly on the grate of the grill and cook until crusty and lightly charred, about 5 minutes. Turn the lamb over and sear the other side, another 5 minutes. Remove the lamb from the grill and let cool slightly. If using gas, reduce the heat to medium; if using charcoal, keep the grill open to let it cool down slightly.

3. Once the lamb is cool enough to handle, about 5 minutes, skewer it onto the rotisserie rod. Start the rotisserie and cook for 1 hour. (If using charcoal, add 2 dozen coals to the fire after about 45 minutes of cooking time.)

4. Brush the lamb all over with the glaze. Cook for another 15 to 30 minutes, basting often with the glaze, until cooked to medium-rare (page 5); the internal temperature should be about 145 degrees F on an instant-read thermometer. Remove the lamb from the grill, baste again with the glaze, and let rest for 20 minutes. Leave the grill on.

5. Brush the onion slices with oil and grill for 5 minutes. Turn them over carefully (making sure they do not separate) and cook until sweet and softened, about 5 minutes more. Separate into rings and set aside.

6. Place the wrapped tortillas on the grill. Close the cover and let heat through, about 5 minutes.

7. Slice the lamb across the grain into $\frac{1}{4}$-inch-thick slices. Serve immediately, folded into warm tortillas with goat cheese, shredded romaine, grilled red onions, and tomato salsa.

Serves 8 to 10

BOBBY
FLAY'S
BOY
GETS
GRILL

224

Grilled Lamb Chops with Garlic, Fresh Thyme, and Grilled Lemons

A simple but satisfying main dish, these thick lamb chops are perfumed with the aromatics of the Mediterranean—lemon, garlic, and thyme. I'd serve this with one of my Greek-inspired yogurt dips, Grilled Vegetable–Saffron Rice Salad (page 78), and Grilled Zucchini with Romesco Sauce and Hazelnuts (page 74).

When shopping for this recipe, I always look for domestic lamb, even though imported lamb from New Zealand and Australia has also become popular. Domestic lamb cuts are larger and often more flavorful.

**BEEF,
LAMB,
PORK,
AND
SAUSAGES**

225

½ cup extra-virgin olive oil,
    plus extra for brushing
6 cloves garlic, finely chopped
8 sprigs fresh thyme
8 (4- to 6-ounce) lamb rib chops
Salt and freshly ground black pepper
4 lemons, cut crosswise in half

1. Combine the oil, garlic, and thyme in a shallow large dish or a thick, sealable plastic bag. Add the chops and turn to coat. Cover and refrigerate for about 1 hour. Remove the chops from the refrigerator 20 minutes before grilling.

2. Heat your grill to high (page 3). Season the chops on both sides with salt and pepper.

3. Grill the chops until lightly charred and crusty, 4 to 5 minutes. Turn the chops over, reduce the heat to medium or move to a cooler part of the grill, and grill until just cooked through (page 5), 3 to 4 minutes more.

4. Brush the cut sides of the lemons with oil and grill cut side down until lightly charred, 3 to 5 minutes. Serve immediately, placing 2 chops and 2 lemon halves on each plate.

Serves 4; can be doubled for 6 to 8 (no need to double the marinade)

Grilled Baby Lamb Chops with Orange-Mint Yogurt Sauce and Grilled Oranges

**BOBBY
FLAY'S
BOY
GETS
GRILL**

226

One sure sign of spring in Astoria, New York's biggest Greek neighborhood, is the fresh lamb arriving at the butcher shops and restaurants. I love how the little chops are just oiled up, tossed on the grill, and served spitting hot with a little lemon and black pepper. Lamb and lemon are the classic Greek combination, but I like a little sweetness with red meat, so I played around with orange and dreamed up this delicious yogurt sauce. A creamy sauce that isn't too rich is perfect with lamb, especially with lightly charred orange sections to squeeze over the meat.

Sometimes I like to serve small lamb chops that guests can eat as finger food; New Zealand or other baby rib chops are perfect. If possible, have a butcher "french" them, removing all the fat and sinew from the top of the bones, to make them easy to hold. But regular lamb chops will be good too.

FOR THE SAUCE:

1 cup thick yogurt (page 12)

2 teaspoons finely grated orange zest

¼ cup fresh orange juice

4 cloves garlic, finely chopped

2 tablespoons finely chopped fresh mint leaves

Salt and freshly ground black pepper

Stir all the ingredients together and refrigerate for at least 30 minutes before serving. *(The sauce can be made a few hours in advance, covered, and kept refrigerated.)*

FOR THE CHOPS:

12 (4-ounce) baby lamb chops

Olive oil

Salt and freshly ground black pepper

1 orange, halved

Chopped fresh mint leaves

---

1. Heat your grill to high (page 3).

2. Brush the chops on both sides with oil and season with salt and pepper. Grill until lightly charred and crusty, 3 minutes. Turn the chops over, reduce the heat to medium or move to a cooler part of the grill, and grill until just cooked through (page 5), 2 to 3 minutes more.

3. At the same time, grill the orange halves cut side down until heated through and lightly charred, 3 to 5 minutes. Remove and cut each half in half.

4. Serve the chops immediately, garnishing each plate with yogurt sauce, an orange quarter, and fresh mint. Squeeze the oranges over the chops before eating.

Serves 4; can be doubled for 6 to 8

Roast Leg of Lamb Marinated in Red Chile, Citrus, and Thyme

BOBBY
FLAY'S
BOY
GETS
GRILL

228

Boneless leg of lamb is one of my favorite summer entrées: I love to eat it, and I love how people are so impressed by that big, Flintstone-size hunk of meat. Plus it absorbs flavors well, stays juicy on the grill, and makes fabulous leftovers for sandwiches and salads.

This recipe brings the flavors of New Mexico to the table with three different dried chiles adding sweet, spicy, earthy, and woodsy flavors to the marinade. See page 287 for a good place to buy them. Serve the dish with Grilled Corn on the Cob with Garlic Butter, Fresh Lime, and Queso Fresco (page 70), and Grilled Artichokes with Smoky Tomato Vinaigrette (page 72) as an appetizer.

2 dried ancho chiles, stems and seeds removed

3 dried New Mexico chiles, stems and seeds removed

3 dried cascabel chiles, stems and seeds removed

3 cups orange juice, preferably fresh

½ cup fresh lime juice

1 small red onion, coarsely chopped

3 cloves garlic, chopped

2 tablespoons chopped fresh thyme leaves

Salt and freshly ground black pepper

1 (7-pound) boneless leg of lamb, rolled and tied (someone at the butcher counter can do this for you)

4 oranges, halved

Mild vegetable oil, such as canola

1. Coarsely chop the chiles. Place them in a blender with the orange and lime juices and blend until smooth. Add the onion, garlic, and thyme and blend until smooth. Season to taste with salt and pepper.

2. Place the lamb in a large dish, pour the marinade over it, and turn to coat. Cover and refrigerate for at least 4 hours and up to overnight. Remove from the refrigerator at least 30 minutes before grilling to allow the meat to come to room temperature.

3. Heat your grill to medium-high (page 3).

4. Remove the lamb from the marinade and season all over with salt and pepper. Sear the lamb until browned and crusty, 4 to 5 minutes on each side. Remove the lamb from the grill and let cool slightly.

5. Once the lamb is cool enough to handle, about 5 minutes, skewer it onto the rotisserie rod. Start the rotisserie, close the grill hood, and cook for 1 hour. (If using charcoal, add 2 dozen coals to the fire after about 45 minutes of cooking time.)

6. Cook for another 15 to 30 minutes until medium-rare (page 5). (The internal temperature should be 140 to 150 degrees F as measured on an instant-read thermometer.) Remove from the grill and let rest for 10 minutes. Leave the grill on.

7. While the lamb is resting, brush the the cut sides of the oranges with oil and grill cut side down until heated through and lightly charred, 3 to 5 minutes.

8. Cut the lamb against the grain into ½-inch-thick slices. Serve immediately, garnished with orange halves. Squeeze the juice over the meat before eating.

Serves 8 to 10

Grilled Pork Tenderloin à la Rodriguez with Guava Glaze and Orange-Habanero Mojo

My good friend Eddie Rodriguez, a clothing designer (he is the Rodriguez in Wilke-Rodriguez), is my longtime guide to the wonderful world of Cuban flavor. This recipe is my tribute to him. Lime, orange, garlic, cumin, vinegar, and just the right amount of chile heat are, to me, what make Cuban food so irresistible. If you've never tasted a real Cuban mojo, the classic sauce for pork, plantains, and a lot of other staples, prepare to be blown away.

I like to grill pork tenderloins, which cook fast and stay juicy. Lean pork tenderloins cook like chicken breasts. They're very simple and very tender, but you have got to get them off the grill before they overcook. As soon as they firm up, they are DONE.

FOR THE GLAZE:

1 cup guava jelly (available at Latin
    and Caribbean markets) or apricot jam
¼ cup Dijon mustard
¼ cup orange juice, preferably fresh
Salt and freshly ground black pepper

Whisk the ingredients together and season to taste with salt and pepper. *(The glaze can be made a few days in advance, covered, and kept refrigerated. Bring to room temperature before using.)*

FOR THE MOJO:

2 tablespoons mild vegetable oil,
    such as canola
1 small red onion, finely chopped
4 cloves garlic, finely chopped
3 cups orange juice
½ cup fresh lime juice

½ habanero chile, seeded and finely chopped
2 tablespoons chopped fresh cilantro leaves
1 teaspoon cumin seeds
Salt and freshly ground black pepper

Heat the oil in a saucepan over medium-high heat. Add the onion and garlic and cook, stirring, until soft, about 5 minutes; do not brown. Add the orange juice, lime juice, and habanero and bring to a boil. Cook until reduced by half. Whisk in the cilantro and cumin and season to taste with salt and pepper. *(The mojo can be made a few hours in advance and set aside at room temperature.)*

FOR THE PORK:
2 pork tenderloins, about 1½ pounds each
2 tablespoons mild vegetable oil, such as canola
Salt and freshly ground black pepper

1. Heat your grill to high (page 3). Set aside a few tablespoons of glaze for brushing the cooked pork.

2. Brush the pork with the oil and sprinkle with salt and pepper. Grill, brushing often with the glaze, until just cooked through (page 5), 4 to 5 minutes per side.

3. Remove the pork from the grill, brush with the reserved glaze, and let rest for 10 minutes. Cut into ½-inch-thick slices and arrange on a serving platter. Drizzle with mojo and serve immediately.

Serves 6; can be doubled for 10 or 12 (no need to double the glaze or the mojo)

Asian Spice–Rubbed Pork Chops with Wild Mushroom–Soy Vinaigrette

BOBBY
FLAY'S
BOY
GETS
GRILL

232

I would never have known that wild mushrooms grow all over New York State—and even right here in New York City—if it weren't for the mushroom sellers at the green-markets. Golden chanterelles from upstate are my local favorites, but you can use any mushrooms in this recipe; they're marinated in garlic and soy, then piled on top of a thick pork chop that's infused with the sweet fire of an Asian spice rub. Use the best mushrooms you can find, and this will be as elegant a dish as any you've had in a restaurant.

A great place to buy all kinds of exotic mushrooms is *www.earthydelights.com*.

FOR THE RUB:

2 tablespoons sweet paprika

1 tablespoon dry mustard

2 teaspoons salt

2 teaspoons freshly ground
    black pepper

2 teaspoons ground star anise

2 teaspoons ground ginger

1 teaspoon ground allspice

¼ teaspoon cayenne

Combine all the ingredients in a bowl or a jar with a tight-fitting lid, and mix well. (*The rub keeps well for months stored at room temperature in a jar with a tight-fitting lid.*)

FOR THE MUSHROOMS:

½ cup plus 3 tablespoons peanut oil

1 large shallot, thinly sliced

1 (1-inch) piece fresh ginger, peeled
    and minced

3 cloves garlic, finely chopped

1 pound assorted mushrooms,
    such as chanterelle, cremini,
    stemmed shiitake, oyster, thinly sliced

2 tablespoons soy sauce

¼ cup rice vinegar

2 tablespoons honey

1 tablespoon toasted sesame oil

Salt and freshly ground black pepper

2 tablespoons chopped fresh cilantro leaves

BEEF,
LAMB,
PORK,
AND
SAUSAGES

233

1. Heat 3 tablespoons of the peanut oil in a large skillet over medium-high heat. Add the shallot, ginger, and garlic and cook, stirring, until soft, about 5 minutes; do not brown. Raise the heat to high and add the mushrooms. Cook, stirring often, until soft, about 8 minutes more. (The mushrooms will give off a lot of liquid, but the high heat will help cook it away.)

2. Whisk the soy sauce, vinegar, honey, and sesame oil together in a large bowl. Gradually whisk in the remaining ½ cup peanut oil and season to taste with salt and pepper. Gently mix in the mushrooms (with their liquid) and cilantro. Taste for salt and pepper and set aside at room temperature. *(The mushrooms can be made a few hours in advance and set aside at room temperature.)*

FOR THE PORK:

4 (10-ounce) center cut bone-in
     double pork chops

Mild vegetable oil, such as canola

1. Heat your grill to high (page 3).

2. Brush the chops with oil and rub on one side with plenty of the spice rub. Grill the chops rub side down until lightly charred and crusty, 4 to 5 minutes. Turn the chops over, reduce the heat to medium or move to a cooler part of the grill, close the grill hood, and grill until just cooked through (page 5), 6 to 7 minutes longer.

3. Remove the chops from the grill and let rest for 5 minutes before serving. Transfer to serving plates and spoon some of the mushroom salad over each chop. Serve immediately.

Serves 4; can be doubled for 6 to 8

Pork Chops with Soy-Honey Glaze and Grilled Sweet Onions

BOBBY
FLAY'S
BOY
GETS
GRILL

234

This dish has traveled pretty far from my mom's pork chops with applesauce, but it's basically the same. Pork is great with a little sweetness. Vidalia onions are almost as sweet as apples, and they grill up nicely, since all those natural sugars caramelize quickly over high heat. The strong tastes of sweet and salty in the glaze balance each other perfectly. You end up with a lot of flavor from almost no effort—and what's better than that?

Serve alongside Grilled Potato Salad with Watercress, Scallions, and Blue Cheese Vinaigrette (page 84).

½ cup honey
¼ cup soy sauce
Pinch of hot red pepper flakes
Freshly ground black pepper
8 (4- to 6-ounce) center-cut boneless pork chops,
    cut ½ inch thick
Mild vegetable oil, such as canola
Salt
2 large sweet onions, such as Vidalia
    or Walla Walla, sliced ½ inch thick

1. Combine the honey, soy, and pepper flakes in a small bowl and season to taste with pepper.

2. Heat your grill to high (page 3).

3. Brush the chops on both sides with oil and season with salt and pepper. Set aside a few tablespoons of glaze for brushing the cooked chops.

4. Grill the pork chops until lightly charred and crusty, 4 to 5 minutes. Turn the chops over, reduce the heat to medium or move to a cooler part of the grill, and grill, brushing often with the glaze, until just cooked through (page 5), 3 to 4 minutes more. Remove the chops to a platter and brush with the reserved glaze.

5. Brush the onion slices with oil and season with salt and pepper. Grill the slices until browned, 3 to 4 minutes per side. Serve the chops with the onions on the side.

Serves 4; can be doubled for 6 to 8

Thin Pork Chops
with Fresh Nectarine-Ginger Chutney

A superfast entrée you can put on top of a bowl of fluffy white rice and serve with a big green salad for a light, flavor-packed dinner. The chops should be on the grill for as short a time as possible to keep them from drying out. (Pork is bred to be very lean these days, but I miss those natural fats that keep the meat juicy as it cooks.) When they're ready, the chops will feel bouncy, like a trampoline, when you press them with your finger.

FOR THE CHUTNEY:
2 tablespoons mild vegetable oil,
    such as canola
1 medium red onion, finely chopped
2 cloves garlic, finely chopped
1 (2-inch) piece fresh ginger, peeled
    and minced
1 cup orange juice, preferably fresh
¼ cup red wine vinegar
2 tablespoons dark brown sugar
8 nectarines, pitted and cut
    into ¼-inch-thick slices
¼ cup chopped fresh cilantro leaves
Salt and freshly ground black pepper

1. Heat the oil in a medium saucepan over high heat. Add the onion, garlic, and ginger and cook, stirring, until soft, 8 to 10 minutes; do not brown. Add the orange juice, vinegar, and sugar and cook until reduced by half.

2. Stir in half of the nectarine slices and cook for 3 to 4 minutes. Turn off the heat and stir in the remaining nectarines and the cilantro. Season to taste with salt and pepper. Set aside at room temperature. *(The chutney can be made a few hours in advance, covered, and kept refrigerated. Bring to room temperature before serving.)*

8 bone-in pork chops, cut less than ½ inch thick

Olive oil

Salt and freshly ground black pepper

1. Heat your grill to high (page 3).

2. Brush the chops on both sides with oil and season with salt and pepper. Grill until golden brown and just cooked through (page 5), 2 to 3 minutes per side.

3. Remove the chops from the grill, top with chutney, and serve immediately.

Serves 4; can be doubled for 6 to 8

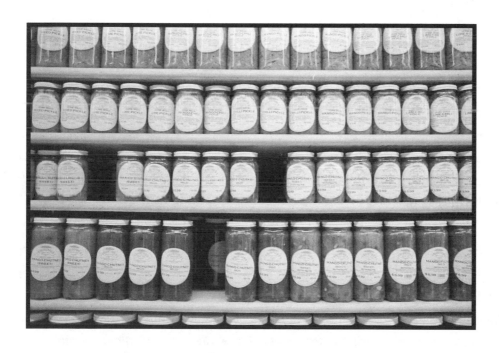

Grilled Bacon, Lettuce, Green Tomato, and Goat Cheese Sandwich

BOBBY
FLAY'S
BOY
GETS
GRILL

238

The classic BLT is my favorite sandwich, hands down, but that doesn't mean that the B can't be grilled and the T has to be red (I'm always playing around with the basic combination of salty, smoky, rich, and tangy flavors). Green tomatoes are much more tart than red ones, so I've added some creamy goat cheese to this sandwich to keep the flavors in balance. If you've never tried green tomatoes any way other than fried, here's your chance! A combination of red and green tomato slices is delicious too.

16 thick slices bacon

**8 thick slices white bread, preferably from
    a fresh Pullman loaf**

Olive oil

Salt and freshly ground black pepper

8 ounces soft fresh goat cheese

**4 large romaine lettuce leaves, cut crosswise
    in half**

2 green tomatoes, thinly sliced

1. Heat your grill to medium (page 3).

2. Place the strips of bacon on the grill (lay them across the grate so they don't fall through) and grill for 3 to 4 minutes on each side, until golden brown and slightly crispy. Remove the bacon to a plate lined with paper towels.

3. Brush the bread on both sides with oil and season with salt and pepper. Grill the bread for 30 seconds on each side. Remove from the grill and spread the goat cheese on 4 slices of the bread.

4. While the bread is still warm, divide the bacon, lettuce, and tomatoes on top of the goat cheese (you may not use all the tomatoes). Place the remaining bread slices on top and press down lightly to bring the flavors together. Serve immediately.

Serves 4; can be doubled for 6 to 8

Maple-Peach-Glazed Ham Steak

Brunch is my weakness. I love it all—Bloody Marys, eggs, bacon, hollandaise, muffins, mimosas, waffles—and when I'm cooking brunch at my house, I do it all outside. It's easy to make scrambled eggs in a skillet, toast blueberry muffins, and glaze a beautiful ham steak, all on the grate of a hot grill, especially if you're drinking an Extra-Spicy Bloody Mary (page 17) at the time.

This recipe will work with any ham steak, but it's always worth seeking out real American country ham, for the flavor is incomparable. Try *www.country-ham.com*. Taste it before cooking; some hams are very salty. If yours tastes too salty, soak it overnight in water before cooking.

**BEEF,
LAMB,
PORK,
AND
SAUSAGES**

239

1 cup peach preserves
¼ cup pure maple syrup
3 tablespoons orange juice, preferably fresh
1 tablespoon ancho chile powder
Salt and coarsely ground black pepper
1 (1½-pound) ham steak, cut 2 inches thick

1. Stir the preserves, syrup, orange juice, and ancho powder together in a medium bowl. Season to taste with salt and pepper; you want the mixture to be pretty peppery.

2. Heat your grill to high (page 3).

3. Place the ham on the grill, close the cover, reduce the heat to medium, and grill for 8 to 10 minutes on each side, basting with the glaze every few minutes.

4. When the ham is heated through and nicely glazed, remove it to a platter, brush once more with the glaze, and let rest for 5 minutes. Cut into ½-inch-thick slices and serve immediately.

Serves 4; can be doubled for 6 to 8 (no need to double the glaze)

Beer-Simmered Bratwurst
with Grilled Onions and Red Sauerkraut

BOBBY
FLAY'S
BOY
GETS
GRILL

240

My favorite dish for autumn grilling or a tailgate party takes only a little more effort than plain hot dogs but is so much more delicious. Bratwursts are usually precooked, like hot dogs, so grilling crisps them up and makes them juicy. A quick, homemade sauerkraut is very easy to make; I like mine a little sweet and spicy. I've infused the whole dish with warm spices—mustard, coriander, ginger, and caraway—to make your guests sit up and take notice. This dish is better than your average dog!

FOR THE SAUERKRAUT:

2 cups red wine vinegar

1 cup water

¼ cup sugar

**1 large head red cabbage, cored
and thinly shredded**

2 cloves garlic, thinly sliced

1 teaspoon whole mustard seeds

Salt and freshly ground black pepper

Combine the vinegar, water, and sugar in a large saucepan (not aluminum or cast-iron), bring to a boil, reduce the heat, and simmer until the sugar has dissolved. Add the remaining ingredients and simmer until the cabbage is soft, about 20 minutes. Season to taste with salt and pepper. *(The sauerkraut can be made up to 2 days in advance, cooled, covered, and kept refrigerated. Bring to room temperature and drain before serving.)*

FOR THE BRATWURST:

3 large onions, thinly sliced

**3 pounds precooked bratwurst,
pricked with a fork**

6 (12-ounce) bottles dark beer

2 cups water

1 teaspoon coriander seeds

1 teaspoon caraway seeds

1 teaspoon mustard seeds

1 (1-inch) piece fresh ginger, peeled
and chopped

Hot dog buns, hoagie buns, or bratwurst buns

Various mustards (I like spicy brown,
sweet-hot, and coarse-grain)

---

1. Arrange the onion slices on the bottom of a medium stockpot. Place the bratwurst on top and add the beer, water, coriander, caraway, mustard seeds, and ginger. Bring to a simmer and cook for about 10 minutes. Remove from the heat and set aside for at least 10 minutes and up to 1 hour.

2. When ready to serve, heat your grill to high (page 3).

3. Lift the sausages out of the pot. Remove the onions with a slotted spoon and place in a serving bowl. Discard the remaining liquid and aromatics.

4. Grill the sausages until crisp and golden brown on all sides, about 10 minutes total. If you like, grill the buns until lightly toasted. Serve the bratwurst on the buns with sauerkraut, onions, and mustard.

Serves 6; can be doubled for 10 or 12

**BEEF,
LAMB,
PORK,
AND
SAUSAGES**

241

SIMPLE DESSERTS

Watermelon Slices
with Lime-Honey Syrup

If you like attention, try carrying a whole watermelon through Times Square at rush hour! That's what I ended up doing for one cookout. I would do a lot more than that for the perfect watermelon—to me, it's the taste of summer. For an even juicier experience, drizzle this lime syrup on the cold, sweet fruit. Simple and refreshing.

1 cup fresh lime juice
¼ cup honey
1 ripe watermelon, about 12 pounds,
     chilled, quartered lengthwise, and cut
     into thick slices

1. Combine the lime juice and honey in a saucepan. Bring to a boil and cook for 2 minutes. Remove from the heat and chill until ready to serve. *(The syrup can be made up to a day in advance and kept refrigerated.)*

2. Place the watermelon slices on a large platter and drizzle with the syrup. Serve immediately.

Serves about 12

Grilled Nectarines with Blue Cheese, Honey, and Black Pepper

I've served this delicious combination as an appetizer, as a side dish, and as a dessert (not at the same meal, of course). The honeyed, peppery flavors, melting blue cheese, and soft, juicy fruit make it luscious but not overly sweet.

Between New York City's cheese shops, farmers' markets, restaurants, and wine bars, I've learned so much about blues from Denmark, Spain, Italy, France, and even Iowa—all without ever leaving the city!

6 ripe large nectarines, halved and pitted
Mild vegetable oil, such as canola
½ cup crumbled blue cheese
¼ cup honey
Coarsely ground black pepper

1. Heat your grill to high (page 3).

2. Brush the cut sides of the nectarines with oil. Grill cut side down until caramelized and browned, about 2 minutes. Turn the nectarines over and grill for 1 to 2 minutes more, until the flesh is almost soft.

3. Place the nectarines cut side up on a platter and divide the cheese among the cavities. Drizzle with the honey and grind fresh pepper over the top. Serve immediately.

Serves 4; can be doubled for 6 to 8

Grilled Peaches with Crème Fraîche and Molasses

Molasses is the stuff that makes brown sugar brown, and I really like that roasted, intense flavor (see Blueberry Cobbler with Brown Sugar Whipped Cream [page 250], or Rum–Brown Sugar–Glazed Shrimp with Lime and Cilantro [page 114] for proof of my addiction to brown sugar). Molasses gives a little caramel edge to sweet fruit like peaches, and it has a darkness to it that's great with creamy, innocent treats like crème fraîche and vanilla ice cream. If you're not a fan of molasses, try melted bittersweet chocolate in this recipe for the same effect.

This is an extremely easy but pretty sophisticated dessert.

8 ripe peaches, halved and pitted
Mild vegetable oil, such as canola
1 cup crème fraîche or sour cream
¼ cup molasses, light or dark (not blackstrap)

1. Heat your grill to high (page 3).

2. Brush the cut sides of the peaches with oil. Grill cut side down until caramelized and browned, about 2 minutes. Turn the peaches over and grill for 1 to 2 minutes more, until the flesh is almost soft.

3. Place the peaches cut side up on a plate. Drop a tablespoon of crème fraîche in the cavity of each half. Using the tines of a fork or a squeeze bottle, drizzle lightly with molasses. Serve immediately.

Serves 6 to 8

Grilled Pineapple with Butter-Rum Glaze and Vanilla Mascarpone

BOBBY
FLAY'S
BOY
GETS
GRILL

248

Ripe pineapple, with its plentiful natural sugars, is ideal for grilling, and it screams "tropical" like nothing else. This makes a great dessert after spicy Latin, Indian, or Caribbean food. Make sure to let the slices brown; you want lots of those caramelized, almost burnt edges.

Mascarpone is a smooth Italian dairy product with a texture somewhere between whipped cream and cream cheese. It's used in tiramisù and available in many supermarkets and gourmet stores, but if you can't find it, good-quality vanilla ice cream will taste just fine.

1 cup dark rum

12 tablespoons (1½ sticks) unsalted butter

¼ cup light brown sugar

1 vanilla bean

8 ounces mascarpone

1 ripe pineapple, peeled and sliced into ¼-inch-thick rounds

½ cup fresh blueberries

1. Combine the rum, butter, and sugar in a small saucepan and simmer, whisking often, until the sugar has melted and the mixture is slightly thickened, about 10 minutes. *(The glaze can be made a few days in advance, cooled, covered, and kept refrigerated. Bring to room temperature before using.)*

2. Cut the vanilla bean lengthwise in half and scrape out the seeds with the tip of a sharp knife. Whisk the mascarpone and vanilla seeds together. *(The mascarpone can be made a day in advance, covered, and kept refrigerated.)*

3. Heat your grill to high (page 3).

4. Grill the pineapple slices, brushing frequently with the glaze, until browned, 2 to 3 minutes per side.

5. Remove the pineapple to a platter or serving plates and top each slice with a dollop of vanilla mascarpone. Garnish with a few fresh blueberries. Serve immediately.

Serves 6; can be doubled for 10 or 12 (no need to double the glaze)

Blueberry Cobbler
with Brown Sugar Whipped Cream

BOBBY
FLAY'S
BOY
GETS
GRILL

250

A few of my favorite things—blueberries, warm biscuits, whipped cream, and brown sugar—all together in one bowl. I may be a city boy, but I love country desserts like this one. To me, this cobbler is the reason blueberries were put on earth! Baking the biscuits separately from the fruit means that they stay nice and crusty. It also makes the recipe simpler: You can make the biscuits the day before and assemble the cobbler quickly.

FOR THE BISCUITS:

2 cups all-purpose flour

3 tablespoons granulated sugar

1 tablespoon baking powder

1 teaspoon salt

**8 tablespoons (1 stick) unsalted butter,
    cold, cut into pieces**

**¾ cup light cream, plus 2 tablespoons
    to brush on top of biscuits**

1 large egg

**2 tablespoons turbinado or raw sugar
    or 1 tablespoon granulated sugar**

1. Preheat the oven to 350 degrees F. Line a cookie sheet with parchment paper or non-stick baking mats, or use a nonstick cookie sheet.

2. Sift together the flour, granulated sugar, baking powder, and salt in a large bowl. Cut the butter into the flour mixture, rubbing them together with your fingers or a pastry cutter, until the mixture is crumbly and sandy. Whisk the ¾ cup cream and the egg together; add to the flour mixture and stir just until the dough comes together.

3. Roll or pat the dough out ½ inch thick on a lightly floured surface. Using a biscuit or cookie cutter, cut into eight 2-inch circles. Transfer to the prepared cookie sheet. Brush the tops with cream, sprinkle with turbinado sugar, and bake until barely golden brown and still undercooked, 10 to 12 minutes. (*The biscuits can be made up to this point a day in advance. Let cool and store in an airtight container.*)

FOR THE COBBLER:

3 pints fresh blueberries

¼ cup sugar

2 tablespoons fresh lemon juice

2 tablespoons all-purpose flour

1. Preheat the oven to 375 degrees F. Butter a 9-inch square baking dish.

2. Mix together the blueberries, sugar, lemon juice, and flour in a large bowl and let sit for 15 minutes.

3. Pour the mixture into the prepared dish, arrange the biscuits on top, and place the baking dish in the oven (put a rimmed baking sheet on a lower rack to catch any overflow). Bake until the mixture begins to bubble and the biscuits are golden brown, 25 to 30 minutes.

4. Remove from the oven and let cool for 30 minutes before serving.

FOR THE WHIPPED CREAM:

1 cup heavy cream, very cold

2 tablespoons light brown sugar

1 teaspoon vanilla extract

Whip all the ingredients together until soft peaks form. Spoon the cobbler into bowls and top with whipped cream.

Serves 8

Crushed Blackberry Sundaes with Toasted Pecans, Caramel Sauce, and Whipped Cream

One of my first jobs was at a Baskin-Robbins ice cream parlor on the East Side, where I used to go a little crazy with the sundae toppings. I was only fifteen, but I was determined to find the perfect combination. It took a long time, and you can't get it at Baskin-Robbins, but this is it: homemade caramel sauce, real blackberries, and freshly toasted pecans over vanilla ice cream. You'll be glad you took the extra steps to make the sauce and toast the pecans, I promise.

FOR THE SAUCE:

1 cup heavy cream

½ vanilla bean, split lengthwise, seeds scraped out with the tip of a small knife

1½ cups sugar

½ cup water

1 tablespoon unsalted butter, cold

Pinch of salt

1. Combine the cream and vanilla bean and seeds in a small saucepan and bring to a simmer over medium heat. Turn off the heat.

2. In another saucepan, whisk together the sugar and water over high heat. Simmer until dark golden brown, 10 to 12 minutes.

3. Remove the caramel from the heat and carefully (the mixture will splatter) add the vanilla-infused cream, stirring constantly with a wooden spoon. Place over medium heat and cook just until smooth. Remove from the heat, fish out the vanilla bean, and stir in the butter and salt. *(The caramel sauce can be made up to 2 days in advance and kept refrigerated. Rewarm in the top of a double boiler or in the microwave at low heat.)*

FOR THE BLACKBERRIES:

2 pints blackberries

¼ cup sugar

¼ cup cassis (blackcurrant) liqueur (optional)

Combine the blackberries, sugar, and cassis in a medium bowl. Let sit at room temperature for 30 minutes, then crush the berries gently with a fork.

FOR THE SUNDAES:

1 quart vanilla ice cream

1 cup pecans, toasted (page 10) and coarsely chopped

1 cup heavy cream, whipped to soft peaks

Place a scoop of ice cream in individual parfait glasses and top with a drizzle of caramel sauce, a spoonful of crushed blackberries, and a sprinkle of pecans. Repeat until the glasses are full, then top with a large dollop of whipped cream. Serve immediately.

Serves 6; can be doubled for 10 or 12 (no need to double the caramel or the berries)

Fresh Mango *Batidos*

BOBBY
FLAY'S
BOY
GETS
GRILL

254

Long before the smoothie craze swept the country, New Yorkers were sipping luscious tropical *batidos* at their local Latin restaurants. Fruit, ice, and milk whirled together in a blender, *batidos* come in mango and papaya but also more exotic flavors like guava, *guanábana,* and *lulo.*

Mango and vanilla is an even better combination than orange and vanilla, the Creamsicle classic. It's similar but even more soothing and sexy. This smooth shake is perfect after the spicy, charred flavors of grilled food.

24 ounces (3 cups) mango sorbet
12 ounces (1½ cups) vanilla ice cream
2 ripe mangoes, peeled, pitted,
    coarsely chopped
2½ cups whole milk, cold
Fresh mint sprigs

Combine all the ingredients except the mint in a blender and blend until smooth. Divide among 4 glasses, garnish each with a mint sprig, and serve immediately.

Serves 4; can be doubled for 6 to 8

Pineapple-Coconut Milkshakes with Dark Rum

If you like piña coladas . . . this is the dessert for you. Keep all the ingredients very cold until the last minute, then whip up the milkshakes in a blender. The rum, of course, is optional, but I find it very relaxing after grilling a whole meal!

12 ounces (1½ cups) vanilla ice cream

2 cups canned cream of coconut

2 cups diced ripe pineapple,
    preferably fresh

2 cups whole milk, cold

1 cup dark rum

Whipped cream, for topping (optional)

¼ cup sweetened flaked coconut,
    lightly toasted (page 10)

Combine the ice cream, cream of coconut, pineapple, milk, and rum in a blender and blend until smooth. Pour into 4 tall glasses. Top with a dollop of whipped cream and sprinkle with toasted coconut. Serve immediately.

Serves 4; can be doubled for 6 to 8

Café con Leche Milkshakes

Cuban coffee is the best—strong, milky, and sweet. And milkshakes are my favorite way to eat ice cream. You don't even need a spoon—just a beach chair, a glass, and a straw.

I've always loved coffee ice cream; when it's in liquid form and spiked, I am a happy man—I mean, boy!

---

2 cups whole milk, cold
1½ cups strong brewed coffee or espresso,
    chilled
1 pint coffee ice cream
½ cup simple syrup (page 12)
½ cup coffee liqueur
Chocolate-covered espresso beans (optional)

Combine the milk, coffee, ice cream, simple syrup, and liqueur in a blender and blend until smooth. Pour into 4 tall glasses and top with a few chocolate-covered espresso beans. Serve immediately.

Serves 4; can be doubled for 6 to 8

Fresh Blueberry–Vanilla Rum Milkshakes

Most often, when the night is warm and the grill is hot, my dessert cravings involve ice cream. Blueberries, to me, are the taste of summer. Most of my favorite summer meals are designed around tomatoes, lobster, corn, and blueberries, so it's handy to be able to pull a super-easy dessert like this one out of my back pocket. It's like the most delicious smoothie you can imagine.

1½ **cups fresh blueberries**
¼ **cup dark rum**
¼ **cup sugar**
2 **cups whole milk, cold**
1 **pint vanilla ice cream**

1. Combine the blueberries, rum, and sugar in a bowl and let sit at room temperature for 30 minutes.

2. Transfer the blueberry mixture to a blender and add the milk and ice cream. Blend until smooth. Pour into 4 tall glasses and serve immediately.

Serves 4; can be doubled for 8

MENUS

**BOBBY
FLAY'S
BOY
GETS
GRILL**

260

CARIBBEAN, HOT AND SWEET

———

Mojitos (page 21)

Grilled Clams in the Shell (page 105)

*Jerk-Rubbed Chicken Thighs
with Homemade Habanero Hot Sauce (page 168)*

Grilled Split Lobsters with Curry Butter (page 122)

*Pineapple-Coconut Milkshakes
with Dark Rum (page 255)*

When I'm lucky enough to get away from cold, slushy winter to the islands, I don't spend much of my time there behind the stove! Instead I like to check out what the local cooks are doing. It's easy to find them—you just follow the smell of smoke and spice until you find a grill made from an oil drum, set up right on the beach or at the local market. What comes off those grills is amazing. This menu collects my versions of favorite dishes I've had down there, and they all have one thing in common—a haze of delicious, smoky smells.

Shellfish like clams, mussels, and oysters, cooked right on the grate of the grill, are just about the easiest appetizer you can make, and the whiff of smoke makes them taste a little bit exotic. The shells trap the heat so that the shellfish cook in their own briny juices. Then the shells open so you can just slurp them right out. It's real beach food. To adapt the recipe on page 105 for this menu, leave out the ham and sprinkle the opened clams with chopped cilantro and drops of hot sauce instead.

Jerk is the national dish of Jamaica—if it isn't official, it should be—and it's that country's spicy answer to barbecue. It's a similar combination of grilling and smoking but with more sweetness and fire. It's also incredibly easy to make at home. This lobster dish takes me right back to Anguilla, where I first tasted grilled lobster and immediately knew I was onto something big.

GAME PLAN

THE DAY BEFORE:

Make the hot sauce

Make the curry butter

A FEW HOURS BEFORE:

Parcook the lobsters

Rub the chicken

ABOUT AN HOUR BEFORE SERVING:

Light the grill

Make the mojitos

Grill the clams

Grill the chicken

Grill the lobster

Make the milkshakes

Serves 4 (or 8 if all recipes are doubled)

BOBBY
FLAY'S
BOY
GETS
GRILL

262

ENTERTAINING ARGENTINE STYLE

―――――

Rosé Sangria (page 20)

Smoky Red Pepper and White Bean Dip (page 34)

*Black Pepper–Crusted Strip Steaks
with Mint Chimichurri (page 204)*

*Grilled Potato Salad with Watercress, Scallions,
and Blue Cheese Vinaigrette (page 84)*

*Watermelon Slices
with Lime-Honey Syrup (page 245)*

I love the new South American steakhouses that have come to New York City. They're called *churrascarías,* which means that everything is grilled, and the waiters keep coming around with more meat until you beg them to stop. Sometimes you can see and hear the meat cooking in the pit, which always makes me even hungrier. Grilling is huge in Argentina, where the people eat more meat than anywhere else in the world. The basic *asado* is an unlimited amount of perfectly mixed grill, usually with kidneys, sweetbreads, and *morcilla* (blood sausage) tossed on the grill along with steaks. Flavorful cuts like the *churrasco* (skirt steak) and *bistec* (flank steak), even though they're not the tenderest, are the most prized there.

I built this menu around the steaks and, of course, the classic Argentine chimichurri, a garlicky green purée loaded with herbs. The bright, fresh flavor is great with anything grilled, from chicken to vegetables. Roasted potatoes and salad are always served at the *churrascarías;* I put them together in a bowlful of grilled potatoes and crunchy water-cress, sparked with the tang of a mustard vinaigrette and crumbled creamy-sharp blue cheese. When your guests arrive, have the purée of white beans, olive oil, and roasted peppers waiting, and put pieces of flatbread for dipping around the edges of the grill as you cook.

Cool, fresh fruit is the best way to end a summer feast. Watermelon slices can be served plain or drizzled with a mixture of honey and lime juice that makes them a little special. I buy honey at my local greenmarket, where there's a stand offering tastes of all the different flavors. The differences aren't huge, but you can taste a bit of lavender here, a hint of clover there, and it's all part of the fun.

GAME PLAN

THE NIGHT BEFORE OR THE MORNING OF:

Make the sangria

Make the dip

Make the syrup for the watermelon

A FEW HOURS BEFORE:

Make the chimichurri

Marinate the steaks

Boil the potatoes

Slice and refrigerate the watermelon

ABOUT AN HOUR BEFORE SERVING:

Light the grill

Finish the sangria

Finish the potato salad

Grill the steaks

Serves 6 (double the potato salad and halve the watermelon recipe)

BOBBY
FLAY'S
BOY
GETS
GRILL

264

GREEK ON THE GRILL

———

*Grilled Flatbread with Cucumber-Yogurt Salad
and Toasted Walnuts (page 38)*

*Grilled Whole Fish with Oregano Salt
and Black Olive–Feta Relish (page 162)*

*Grilled Baby Lamb Chops with Orange-Mint
Yogurt Sauce and Grilled Oranges (page 226)*

*Grilled Nectarines with Blue Cheese, Honey,
and Black Pepper (page 246)*

No one knows more about grilling than the Greeks. I had already graduated from cooking school and opened my own restaurant when I went to Greece for the first time. I quickly realized that compared with the cooks there I didn't know a thing about grilling fish.

When I came back, I went looking for the *tavernas* in Astoria, a neighborhood in Queens that's home to New York's large Greek community. True, Astoria doesn't look a whole lot like Greece—especially the parts where the subway runs overhead—but a lot of things are the same: the smell of burning charcoal and dark-roast coffee from the restaurants, the big hunks of lamb hanging in the butcher shop windows, the baklava in the bakery windows. And the grilled fish are just as good: juicy, sliding off the bone, steaming olive oil, lemon, and oregano.

Greek food doesn't use a lot of different ingredients, but each one is always totally fresh and the best it can be. This is the time to make the effort to get the freshest fish around and to go to the greenmarket for fresh mint and oregano instead of dried. The payoff will be huge.

GAME PLAN

THE MORNING OF:

Start the flatbread

A FEW HOURS BEFORE:

Make the cucumber-yogurt salad

Make the orange-mint yogurt sauce

Make the black olive–feta relish

ABOUT AN HOUR BEFORE SERVING:

Light the grill

Prepare the fish

Grill the flatbread

Grill the fish

Grill the lamb chops

Grill the nectarines

Serves 6 to 8 (double the fish, lamb, and nectarine recipes)

**BOBBY
FLAY'S
BOY
GETS
GRILL**

266

INDIAN SPICE

Mango-Mint Iced Tea (page 18)

*Brick-Grilled Baby Squid
with Tamarind-Mint Dressing (page 130)*

*Tandoori-Marinated Rotisserie Cornish Hens
(page 193)*

*Coconut-Cashew Basmati Rice Salad
(page 76)*

*Pineapple-Coconut Milkshakes with Dark Rum
(page 255)*

I am hardly an expert on authentic Indian cooking, but like everyone who lives in New York City, I'm often seduced by the rich smells that come pouring out of the many restaurants, delis, and street carts that sell Indian food. I also love the shops in the neighborhood known as Curry Hill, on Lexington Avenue in the upper 20s, with sacks of basmati rice, blocks of tamarind pulp, and usually the scent of a vegetable curry simmering away in the back. This menu takes you a little farther into that melting pot.

Indian food is probably not the first thing that comes to mind when you think "grilling." But a lot of the foods I really like to grill—whole chickens, flatbreads, squid, and vegetables—are cooked in India in a tandoor, a round clay oven with hot charcoal in the bottom. The heat is trapped inside, and the food—which has been marinating in a tangy, spiced yogurt—is grilled on racks set over the white-hot coals. The combination of intense heat, bold spice, and smoky flavor is fabulous. You can easily make a delicious approximation of tandoori on an American grill.

All these recipes are inspired by my favorite thing about Indian cooking—the rich and complex spice mixes, which are really easy to produce. All it takes is a set of measuring spoons! But Indian food is more than spice powders; fresh garlic, cilantro, ginger, mango, pineapple, coconut, mint, and chiles are just a few of the familiar aromatics they use, and that I'm already addicted to in my own cooking.

GAME PLAN

THE NIGHT BEFORE:

Make the tandoori marinade and marinate the hens

THE MORNING OF:

Make the iced tea

A FEW HOURS BEFORE:

Make the tamarind-mint dressing

Make the rice salad

ABOUT AN HOUR BEFORE SERVING:

Light the grill

Grill the squid

Grill the hens

Make the milkshakes

Serves 6 to 8 (double all the recipes except the rice salad)

BOBBY
FLAY'S
BOY
GETS
GRILL

268

SPANISH FIESTA

———

White Peach Sangria (page 19)

Tomato Bread with Prosciutto (page 37)

*Grilled Clams in the Shell with Serrano Ham
(page 105)*

*Grilled Whole Fish with Tarragon, Orange,
and Parsley (page 160)*

*Grilled Vegetable–Saffron Rice Salad
(page 78)*

*Grilled Nectarines with Blue Cheese, Honey,
and Black Pepper (page 246)*

The big flavors of Spain blew me away my first time there, which was long after I became a chef. It was like meeting a bunch of great people who seemed like old friends right away: sweet piquillo peppers, serrano ham, sherry vinegar, Manchego cheese, paprika, garlic, and, of course, the unbelievable golden olive oil. It was easy to see (and taste) the connections between Spanish food and the food I was already cooking at Mesa Grill. Mesa's food has influences from Mexico, the Caribbean, and the American Southwest—all at some point ruled by Spain.

So I came back to New York, cooked up a storm, and opened Bolo in 1994. The Spanish influences on the food there are huge, but I always remember that I'm cooking for New Yorkers. These dishes are lively and complex (food in Spain tends to be very simple, with just a few ingredients) and easy to make on the grill.

The absolute best and simplest tapa in Spain is bread rubbed with a garlic clove, the cut face of a ripe tomato, and drizzled with olive oil; my version is easier to make on the spot for a bunch of people and just as good. Clams with ham, and shellfish with pork in general, is a tradition in Spain and Portugal. It's a strange-sounding but fabulous combination of salty ingredients. Cooking clams on the grill is fun and always very impressive. Aromatics like saffron, sweet-tart sherry vinegar, and refreshing tarragon round out the strong Spanish flavors.

GAME PLAN

THE MORNING OF:

Make the sangria

Make the tomato purée for the bread

Make the vinaigrette for the fish

Make the dressing for the rice salad

A FEW HOURS BEFORE:

Make the rice salad

Stuff the fish with herbs and orange slices; keep refrigerated

Slice the bread for the tomato bread

ABOUT AN HOUR BEFORE SERVING:

Light the grill

Finish the sangria

Make the tomato bread

Grill the clams

Grill the fish

Grill the nectarines

Serves 6 to 8 (double all the recipes except the rice salad)

BOBBY
FLAY'S
BOY
GETS
GRILL

270

CUBAN MOJITO PARTY

———

Mojitos (page 21)

Avocado Salad with Tomatoes, Lime,
and Toasted Cumin Vinaigrette (page 56)

Grilled Pork Tenderloin à la Rodriguez
with Guava Glaze and Orange-Habanero Mojo
(page 230)

Grilled Corn on the Cob with Garlic Butter,
Fresh Lime, and Queso Fresco (page 70)

Fresh Mango Batidos (page 254)

What is it about Cuban food? Why is it so seductive? Even my old friend Eddie Rodriguez, who grew up in Miami, can't quite put his finger on what makes the *sabor cubano* so intoxicating. But he did take me to Union City, New Jersey, the Little Havana neighborhood close to NYC, so that we could try to figure it out together. Even before we ate anything, he was dancing down the sidewalk in anticipation.

To me, Cuban food stands out because of how it puts flavors up against each other—sweet with salty, pork with citrus, garlic with orange, mint with lime, sweet tropical fruit with cream. Like most Caribbean food, it's got a lightness that makes it perfect for hot weather, but it's not nearly as spicy—in terms of chile heat—as some other tropical cuisines. This menu gives you some of the irresistible tastes and smells of Bergenline Avenue, the main drag of Union City's Little Havana, with its open-air fruit and vegetable markets, and the great cooking aromas from all the espresso machines and sandwich presses in the cafés.

Even a simple avocado salad, a *café con leche,* and a ham-and-cheese sandwich (pressed until crisp and melting, of course) taste better in a Cuban café than anywhere else. Try the Pressed Cuban-Style Burger on page 198 too. Finish off with a mango *batido,* if it doesn't finish you off first. I usually have to take a nap after a visit to Little Havana.

GAME PLAN

THE NIGHT BEFORE OR THE MORNING OF:

Make the salad dressing

Make the garlic butter

Make the guava glaze

A FEW HOURS BEFORE:

Make the mojo

ABOUT AN HOUR BEFORE SERVING:

Light the grill

Soak the corn

Make the salad

Make the mojitos

Grill the corn

Grill the pork

Make the *batidos*

Serves 6 (double all the recipes except the pork and corn)

BOBBY
FLAY'S
BOY
GETS
GRILL

272

ITALIAN-AMERICAN
FIREHOUSE DINNER

———

*Fresh Buffalo Mozzarella with Red and Yellow
Tomatoes and Basil Vinaigrette (page 58)*

*Grilled Pizza with Grilled Sausage, Peppers,
Onions, and Oregano Ricotta (page 40)*

*Porterhouse Steaks with Fra Diavolo Barbecue
Sauce and Cherry Pepper Salad (page 206)*

*Grilled Peaches with Crème Fraîche
and Molasses (page 247)*

As everyone in New York knows, our firemen eat really well. We can tell because there are always fire trucks parked outside the city's best markets and usually a few guys in big rubber boots checking out the produce and the meat. So I was very excited when I got called to the station house on Arthur Avenue in the Bronx. It was an honor to cook for these guys, and I wanted to grill them something special that would have a taste of their neighborhood, which is a real old-time Little Italy. Arthur Avenue is lined with stores that still make fresh mozzarella, pasta, focaccia, and sausages by hand. Italian-Americans, and Italian food lovers from all over the city and beyond, come to the neighborhood every Saturday. As they shop, they eat freshly shucked clams from the makeshift clam bar in front of the fish store, eat chunks of bread studded with prosciutto right out of the bag, and stop every few blocks for an espresso and a cannoli.

This menu is a great big blend of American and Italian. Tomato-mozzarella salad is now just as popular here as it is in southern Italy. Same goes for pizza! Thick porterhouse steaks are big in both places, and I brewed a sauce that blends classic barbecue flavors with my favorite "rod sauce," the spicy tomato fra diavolo. Piquant cherry peppers pickled in vinegar are staples in Italian delis in New York; I've made it into a salad for the steak with roasted peppers, cherry tomatoes, and a strong red wine vinaigrette.

GAME PLAN

A FEW DAYS BEFORE:

Make the barbecue sauce

THE MORNING OF:

Make the basil vinaigrette

Make the pizza dough

Make the cherry pepper salad

ABOUT AN HOUR BEFORE SERVING:

Light the grill

Make the tomato-mozzarella salad

Grill the pizza toppings

Grill the pizzas

Grill the steaks

Grill the peaches

Serves 6 to 8 (double the mozzarella and steak recipes)

BOBBY
FLAY'S
BOY
GETS
GRILL

274

Brunch is one of America's great culinary creations. Lots of countries make fried chicken and apple pie, but brunch? Only in America, and I love it. Having muffins, eggs, quesadillas, country ham, and a nice cool cocktail all at the same meal is like a dream come true! In New York, the ritual is to hang out and read the paper on the sidewalk while you wait for a table at the best pancake place or the place with famous cheese grits. For me, inventing new spins on eggs Benedict, French toast, and hash browns for the brunch menu at Mesa Grill is one of the most fun parts of the job.

But inviting friends over to grill on a sunny summer morning is fun too, and very easy. Guests are happy to sit around for a while while you cook. Hand them a section of the newspaper and a Bloody Mary to help work up an appetite. Quesadillas make a nice change for brunch, and this one has the delicious smoky bacon that everyone loves. I'd add some simply scrambled eggs to this menu; making them on the grill is as easy as making them in your kitchen. Just put your skillet right on the grate and let it preheat; you'll have the perfect low temperature for scrambling eggs.

Real Southern country ham, which is cured with sugar and then smoked and aged, is something everyone should taste now and then, no matter where they live. It used to be nearly impossible to get up North, but now, of course, anyone anywhere can find it on the Internet! Try *www.country-ham.com*.

GAME PLAN

THE NIGHT BEFORE:

Make the Bloody Marys

Make the peach glaze

Make the butter-rum glaze

Slice the pineapple

Make the mascarpone

THE MORNING OF:

Make the relish

ABOUT AN HOUR BEFORE SERVING:

Light the grill

Grill the quesadillas

Grill the ham

Grill the pineapple

Serves 4 (or 8 if all the recipes are doubled)

BOBBY
FLAY'S
BOY
GETS
GRILL

276

CHINATOWN MARKET

*Crunchy Vegetable Slaw with Peanut Sauce
and Crispy Noodles (page 66)*

*Grilled Shrimp Skewers with Soy Sauce,
Fresh Ginger, and Toasted Sesame Seeds
(page 116)*

*Peking Duck Breasts with Scallions, Pancakes,
and Grilled Oranges (page 188)*

*Fresh Blueberry–Vanilla Rum Milkshakes
(page 257)*

To New Yorkers who are into food (me included), there's nothing more exciting than discovering a great new Chinese restaurant. When the cravings strike, my friend Patricia Yeo and I head down to Chinatown, where I love to shop for food as well as eat it. With its crowds, top-quality produce, and exotic new foods showing up all the time, Chinatown is one of New York's most energizing neighborhoods. It's fun to be with so many other people who are clearly thinking about my favorite subject—food!

I took some of Patricia's experience with Chinese ingredients to help me adapt these versions of my favorite Chinese dishes to the grill. It may not be the most authentic Chinese food you'll ever eat, but who cares? This menu is all about crunch and contrast. The slaw is a tribute to the tangy-sweet pickled cabbage that Chinatown restaurants often give you to munch on while waiting for your dumplings. And sweet shrimp, salty soy, and grill smoke make an addictive dish.

Duck breast is always one of my favorite things to grill, and since Peking duck is probably my favorite Chinese dish, creating my own version was a pleasure. In that dish, it's the contrast of the cool cucumber, hot duck, salty-sweet hoisin sauce, and soft pancakes that works so incredibly well. Hoisin sauce is flavored with garlic, chiles, and sesame. It's one of the staples of the Chinese kitchen, and its dark, rich, complex flavors remind me of ingredients like balsamic vinegar and chipotle purée. (And like those ingredients, it's a quick way to add a lot of different flavor elements to a dish.)

When I was a kid, we always stopped at Baskin-Robbins on our way home from Chinatown, and I still crave ice cream after Chinese food. A milkshake makes the perfect soothing dessert.

GAME PLAN

THE DAY BEFORE:

Make the peanut sauce

Make the hoisin glaze

A FEW HOURS BEFORE:

Make the slaw

Skewer the shrimp

ABOUT AN HOUR BEFORE SERVING:

Light the grill

Marinate the shrimp

Grill the duck

Grill the oranges and pancakes

Grill the shrimp

Make the milkshakes

Serves 8 (double all the recipes except the vegetable slaw)

ASIAN FLAVORS

———

*Grilled Swordfish with Coconut, Key Lime,
and Green Chile Sauce (page 158)*

*Soy-Ginger Chicken Rolled in Crisp Lettuce
with Peanut Dipping Sauce (page 170)*

*Coconut-Cashew Basmati Rice Salad
(page 76)*

*Watermelon Slices with Lime-Honey Syrup
(page 245)*

When I was growing up in New York, Chinese was the only game in town as far as Asian food was concerned. Now all the local kids grow up eating Vietnamese summer rolls and Thai chicken curry—not to mention lots of sushi! And their parents have become addicted to the ingredients, cuisines, and flavors of Asia. Just in my neighborhood, I can buy fresh Japanese shiso leaves at the greenmarket, I can snack on grilled beef skewers with Thai peanut sauce, and I can order in Vietnamese salads, with huge flavors that always blow me away.

Without trying to get into the "fusion" thing, I've found myself incorporating more and more Asian ingredients into my cooking, especially during the summer. This hot-weather cuisine includes a lot of dishes that are great on the grill. The idea of wrapping hot grilled food in cool lettuce leaves and fresh herbs, as they do in Vietnam, is one of the first ideas I stole for my own cooking! And the ingredients of Southeast Asia—including Malaysia, Thailand, Vietnam, and their neighbors—have a lot in common with the Latin flavors I love: fresh chiles, coconut, cilantro, lime juice, mango, and toasted cumin. Thai and Vietnamese dipping sauces are usually a combination of sugar, salt, vinegar, and chile, so they set off all the flavor receptors in your mouth.

This menu is a super-easy way to introduce some new flavors to your good old backyard grill.

GAME PLAN

THE DAY BEFORE:

Make the lime syrup

Make the soy-ginger glaze

A FEW HOURS BEFORE:

Make the coconut sauce

Make the peanut dipping sauce

Skewer the chicken

Make the rice salad

Slice and refrigerate the watermelon

HALF AN HOUR BEFORE SERVING:

Light the grill

Grill the fish

Grill the chicken

Serves 6 to 8 (double the swordfish and chicken recipes and halve the watermelon recipe)

BOBBY
FLAY'S
BOY
GETS
GRILL

280

SPRING FLING ON THE GRILL

Fava Bean and Manchego Cheese Salad
(page 64)

Grilled Shrimp Taquitos with Asparagus,
Red Cabbage, and Creamy Chipotle Sauce
(page 110)

Grilled Lamb Chops with Garlic, Fresh Thyme,
and Grilled Lemons (page 225)

Crushed Blackberry Sundaes with Toasted Pecans,
Caramel Sauce, and Whipped Cream (page 252)

If you're like me, the arrival of spring has nothing to do with the first bluebird or the first crocus, and everything to do with the first bag of charcoal. By the time warm weather finally rolls in, I can't wait to try out all the new grilling ideas I've been fantasizing about all winter. And the arrival in the markets of new spring ingredients like fava beans, real asparagus, baby beets, red stalks of rhubarb, and fresh domestic lamb always makes me want to get out there and start cooking.

Spring is my favorite season at New York's greenmarkets, which range from a few tents selling apples, flowers, and bread on little Abingdon Square, to the blockbuster Union Square market, which is so large that chefs can actually provision their restaurant kitchens there. Even if the vegetables and fruits are slow to come—March and April are pretty much just new potatoes and onions—the springtime energy is fantastic, as everyone turns up each week hoping for a sighting of the first asparagus and zucchini blossoms.

It's that kind of anticipation that makes "seasonal cooking" such a buzzword among chefs. But I don't like to get too strict about it. If we all really cooked seasonally, winter would be nothing but cabbage soup and boiled potatoes! The pleasure of shopping at your local greenmarket is about more than seasonality—it's about community. In every season, I can buy honey, bread, and even smoked clams at my local greenmarket and enjoy the shopping almost as much as the eating.

GAME PLAN

THE DAY BEFORE:

Make the creamy chipotle sauce

Make the caramel sauce

A FEW HOURS BEFORE:

Cook the fava beans

Make the vinaigrette

Make the cabbage

Marinate the lamb chops

AN HOUR BEFORE SERVING:

Light the grill

Make the salad

Crush the blackberries

Grill the taquitos

Grill the lamb chops

Make the sundaes

Serves 6 (double all the recipes except the sundaes)

BOBBY
FLAY'S
BOY
GETS
GRILL

282

SUMMER ROOFTOP PARTY

———

Rosé Sangria (page 20)

Grilled Bread Panzanella (page 63)

*Cedar-Planked Lobster Tails with Corn
and Smoked Chile Relish (page 128)*

*Grilled Ribeye Steak
with Cilantro-Garlic Butter (page 220)*

*Grilled Peaches with Crème Fraîche
and Molasses (page 247)*

When I walk around Manhattan on a beautiful summer night—on one of those rare occasions when the weather is just perfect—I'm amazed by how many people are actually grilling outside. In the unlikeliest places, you can suddenly smell the unmistakable scent of meat, charcoal, and fire. New Yorkers are so determined to grill that they'll set up a kettle grill on the roof or even stick a miniature hibachi out on the windowsill and cook burgers for dinner. It's really fun, especially because you have the thrill of doing something a little bit illegal.

But New York summers are mostly about getting out of the city and into the country, to the beach, the lake, or wherever you can really enjoy the season. For me, that's got to be a place with plenty of farmstands, like Long Island, where there are still farming families who sell their tomatoes, corn, herbs, zucchini, potatoes, and peaches by the side of the road. But since I love lobster so much, it's also got to be a place with great seafood—like Long Island! The centuries-old fishing tradition of the island's long coastline is still there, especially in fish markets that pride themselves on the freshness and quality of their stock.

Summer cooking should be easy, above all—so if you can't find the cedar planks or the store is out of crème fraîche, don't push it. If you're eating corn, lobster, tomatoes, and peaches, you're having the perfect summer dinner, whatever recipes you use!

GAME PLAN

THE DAY BEFORE:
Make the garlic butter

A FEW HOURS BEFORE:
Make the corn relish
Make the sangria
Soak the cedar planks

HALF AN HOUR BEFORE SERVING:
Light the grill
Finish the sangria
Make the panzanella
Grill the steak
Grill the lobster
Grill the peaches

Serves 8 (double all the recipes except the panzanella and peaches)

BOBBY
FLAY'S
BOY
GETS
GRILL

284

MESA GRILL CLASSICS

———

White Peach Margaritas (page 22)

*Grilled Quesadillas with Sweet Corn,
Grilled Shrimp, and Jalapeño Pesto (page 44)*

*Grilled Sea Scallops
with Papaya-Tomatillo Salsa (page 106)*

*Coffee Spice–Rubbed Ribeye
with Smoky Tomato–Red Chile Salsa (page 216)*

*Blueberry Cobbler
with Brown Sugar Whipped Cream (page 250)*

When we opened in 1991, I could never, ever have dreamed that Mesa Grill would be such a success. Sometimes the right place, the right people, and the right food just make magic, whether it's in a restaurant, in your kitchen, or in your own backyard.

On Mesa's opening day, New York was still infatuated with Southwestern cooking—it was the next new thing after Cajun cooking came to town in the '80s—but that trend is long gone, and Mesa is still standing. In fact, it's roaring.

I like to think that Mesa still works because the food (and drinks) have stayed true to my original menus, without being too literal about it. I've learned a lot about cooking since 1991, but my taste hasn't changed a bit. I still like bold flavor, grilled steaks, fruity cocktails, intense herbs, sweet corn, melted cheese, tender shellfish, smoky bacon, and fiery chiles. I like the energy that comes from cooking for people who are having a good time and, of course, I love it when people really enjoy my food—and show it by coming back year after year. Sometimes now, people who had their first dates at our bar come in with their children for brunch; I can't even say how rewarding that is for us.

These are some of the classics that I've perfected over the years. They are (almost) always on the menu, and now they're as close as you can get to eating at Mesa Grill without leaving your house!

GAME PLAN

THE DAY BEFORE:

Make the spice rub

Make the jalapeño pesto

Make the biscuits for the cobbler

A FEW HOURS BEFORE:

Bake the cobbler

Make the papaya-tomatillo sauce

Make the tomato–red chile salsa

ABOUT AN HOUR BEFORE SERVING:

Light the grill

Make the margaritas

Grill the quesadillas

Grill the scallops

Grill the steaks

Serves 8 (double all the recipes except the cobbler)

Sources

FOR BARBECUE WOOD, CHIPS, AND PLANKS:

www.barbecuewood.com, 509-961-3420

www.justsmokedsalmon.com, 866-716-2710

FOR DRIED CHILES AND HOT SAUCES:

www.kitchenmarket.com, 212-243-4433

FOR SPICES:

www.kalustyan.com, 908-688-6111

FOR CHEESES:

www.dairysection.com

FOR FRESH LOBSTERS:

www.mainelobsterdirect.com, 800-556-2783

www.thelobsternet.com, 800-360-9520

FOR DUCK AND GAME:

www.dartagnan.com, 800-327-8426

FOR ORGANIC CHICKENS:

www.eberlypoultry.com, 717-336-6440

FOR WILD MUSHROOMS:

www.earthydelights.com, 800-367-4709

FOR COUNTRY HAMS:

www.country-ham.com, 888-881-8728

FOR MIDDLE EASTERN AND INDIAN INGREDIENTS:

www.ethnicgrocer.com, 866-438-4642

FOR SPANISH INGREDIENTS, SUCH AS WHITE ANCHOVIES:

www.tienda.com, 888-472-1022

FOR PORTUGUESE INGREDIENTS:

www.amarals.com, 508-993-7645

SOURCES

Index

INDEX

300